# From Anger to Love

A COLLABORATION SPANNING THE FIELDS
OF SCIENCE, PSYCHOLOGY AND
CONTEMPLATIVE TRADITIONS

**Daaji (Kamlesh Patel)**
with
Matthieu Ricard, James Doty, Pir Zia Inayat-Khan,
Llewellyn Vaughan-Lee, Scilla Elworthy, Satish Kumar,
Ruby Carmen, Vasco Gaspar, Marilyn Cornelius,
Victor Kannan and Elizabeth Denley.

First published by Sahaj Marg Spirituality Foundation, India, in 2023

Published by Westland Books, a division of Nasadiya Technologies Private Limited, in 2024

No. 269/2B, First Floor, 'Irai Arul', Vimalraj Street, Nethaji Nagar, Alapakkam Main Road, Maduravoyal, Chennai 600095

Westland and the Westland logo are the trademarks of Nasadiya Technologies Private Limited, or its affiliates.



ISBN: 9789360454678

10 9 8 7 6 5 4 3 2 1



Edited by Elizabeth Denley
Printed at Nutech Print Services, India

# Contents

# Foreword

FERDINAND WULLIEMIER

The circumstances that led me to write this Foreword are significantly related to the subject matter of the book. For weeks, my wife and I could not agree on how to handle the numerous problems we were facing, which had resulted from the tragic suicide of our tenant, who killed herself because of crippling debt.

During one conversation, the pitch and tone of our voices started to change. Feeling anger rising inside of me, I expressed my feeling of being misjudged before immediately leaving the room so as not to ruin the usually warm and courteous relationship between us. In my study, I opened the computer where the first e-mail I found was from the editor of this book, who had sent it at the exact moment of our interaction. It was an invitation to write the Foreword you have started to read!

This true *synchronicity* was an arrow on target, reaching my heart with the magistral and emergent advice to transcend the negative aspect of my deep-rooted anger. I also interpreted it as the connection with my current spiritual guide, telling me, 'Knowing your remaining problem, here is an additional opportunity to transform your residual anger into a healthy and positive dynamic. Accepting to write the Foreword implies that you will read all the chapters of the book with sustained attention and introspection. This will also give you the advantage of being busy, diverting you from your present sorrows.'

Being sensitive to synchronicities and other parapsychological phenomena, I had no choice but to accept without hesitation. It offered me the immediate opportunity to use my anger in a healthy way, that is, to put into practice the title of the book, *From Anger to Love.* The concomitant feeling of being looked after and protected by my guide, who was offering me his help, reinforced my confidence and alleviated the stress my wife and I were feeling.

Reading this book is a valuable gift. I say this not only for myself, but surely for all of us who are motivated to improve our mastery over the negative side of anger and other emotional reactions we are sure to experience in our lives. The different authors have described with honesty and authenticity a wide range of personal experiences, all corresponding with their various level of consciousness and development at given times. Moreover, the authors describe positive personal transformations that resulted from their perseverant and courageous efforts to improve, coupled with the help they received. As happened for me, I'm convinced that you, the reader, will also benefit by identifying with at least one personal story and with one or more of the solutions offered.

Of course, sufferings are surely to be experienced during the more or less unpredictable adventures we have to go through. They are known as the *bhoga* of our *samskaras*, which together constitute our *karma*. Sometimes, such trials are so powerful that we temporarily regress to previous stages of development and vibrational levels. Here again, the authors provide us with encouragement, consolation and reassurance.

In 2010, my spiritual guide asked me, 'You are a psychiatrist. Can you tell me if it is normal to become more irritable as we grow older?' I answered, 'Yes, it is well known, and the present explanation is related to the aging of our brain and the decrease of our reserves of bioenergy. Being 15 years younger than you, I already feel it, maybe because I was already irritable as a young man, partly due to the genetics from my father's side and that is something I have been using as an excuse for many years.' So I find that another very useful aspect of this book is how to use the positive sides of anger.

Let me conclude with a single suggestion: please read this book carefully and diffuse it as widely as you can, because it will help your family members and friends. It contains a large spectrum of bio-psycho-socio-spiritual approaches to anger and other emotions, plus the various ways to handle them in order to gradually progress toward universal love, which is ideally our way of being and living.

*Ferdinand Wulliemier*
12 December 2022, Lausanne, Switzerland

Dr. Wulliemier is a semi-retired psychiatrist who was head of the Liaison Psychiatry Service of the Centre Hospitalier Universitaire (CHU) of Lausanne, teaching both medical and psychology students. He has published numerous scientific articles, first in the psychosomatic field, adding the spiritual dimension when he started to meditate in 1985 in the Za-zen tradition. Since 1987 he has practised Heartfulness meditation, also volunteering his services as a Heartfulness trainer and researcher. He is the author of more than 20 books (most in French), including the most recent, *La spiritualité, moi et les autres, Vers une civilisation du Cœur*, and *Préparons-nous à ce qui nous attend, en commençant par nos soins.*

# Understanding Anger

DAAJI

## About Daaji

Kamlesh Patel, also known as Daaji, is the fourth and current spiritual guide of the Heartfulness movement. He has spent the past four decades training people across the world in Heartfulness meditation and is the author of three bestsellers, *The Heartfulness Way* (with Joshua Pollock), *Designing Destiny* and *The Wisdom Bridge*. He has also written collections in Heartfulness Magazine on the 'Evolution of Consciousness,' 'Ashtanga Yoga,' 'Yogic Psychology,' and 'How to Remove and Create Habits.'

His work has appeared in the *Times of India*, *Economic Times*, *Hindustan Times*, *HuffPost*, *Thrive*, leading TV networks and a number of academic journals. With a background in pharmacy as well as yoga, Daaji gives keynote addresses at conferences and conducts workshops around the world. His passion lies in grassroots efforts, especially in taking meditation to the local communities and students of all regions of the world. Daaji is a hands-on grandfather and enjoys being with his family in Kanha Shanti Vanam, India.

Daaji was awarded the Padma Bhushan from the President of India, in 2024, and is a thought leader and change maker, bringing together the best of the ancient traditions of yoga and modern science to offer a set of remarkable meditative techniques known as Heartfulness.

Daaji's teachings arise from his personal experience, as well many years of research in yogic science, the world's spiritual traditions and scientific advancements. In spreading Heartfulness practices around the world, Daaji is facilitating social transformation and large-scale reform through personal transformation. Heartfulness is reshaping individual lives – bringing self-confidence, wisdom, compassion and peace.

# Daaji

Most of us struggle with anger. Sometimes we hurt others, causing outer tension and conflict and sometimes we hurt ourselves, causing inner tension and conflict. Either way, we usually regret it. This happens because we have not learned the true nature and purpose of anger, nor the means to work with this volatile emotion. Once we understand our patterns better, anger becomes a good friend.

## What is anger?

In its pure form, anger is a charge of energy in our system. It starts in our energy field and spreads to the physical body. In yogic science, anger is one of two emotions that are given to us for our evolution. Those two emotions are *kama* (passion) and *krodha* (anger) and they can never be removed.

How is anger useful? Its purpose is manifold, but here are two very important functions: from an instinctive biological perspective, anger is for survival – it alerts us to danger so that we either fight or flee. From an emotional perspective it alerts us to another type of threat and warns us that something needs to change. It can become a super tool for continuous improvement.

## What triggers anger?

So many things can trigger anger and they arise from both outside and inside. For example, tragic circumstances and events, insults, criticism, unwanted advice, threats, injustice and humiliation are examples of outside triggers. Expectations, desires, wishes and fears trigger us from within. Anger can also surface from deep within and we are not always aware of the source of that past anger, as it has been stored in our subconscious for a very long time, forming a knot of trapped energy. When the knot surfaces, that energy is released.

Anything that triggers the sympathetic nervous system's 'fight or flight response' can result in anger, as our biological evolution has primed us to be ready whenever there is danger. The real problem arises when we see danger in everyday little things.

A common cause of anger is criticism, especially when it is either unjust or unsolicited. Another common cause is unfulfiled expectations. Insistence on their fulfilment intensifies the fire even more, like pouring oil on it. It's important to understand the difference between having an expectation and being insistent on its fulfilment. For example, consider the difference between a child saying, 'I hope Mommy will pick me up from school,' and 'Only Mommy can pick me up from school!' Any insistence fuels anger with greater intensity.

## What are our angry behavioral responses?

When anger arises, we often blame someone or something external, directing our energy outward: 'You make me so angry!' 'Why did you do that?' The external stimulus may be the trigger, but the reaction is within us. For example, when something goes wrong in a marriage, we often blame our partner. How many of us are honest enough to look at our own imperfections and personal weaknesses instead?

Sometimes we do beat ourselves up: 'I am so hopeless! I keep making the same stupid mistake again and again.' When the blame game turns inward, it can also be destructive, reinforcing the same unhealthy patterns.

Whether we become aggressive or defensive or hurt depends upon our patterns, but what if we could respond differently? What if we could pause and consider the event as an opportunity to learn something about ourselves? Take the example of criticism; we don't have to agree with the other person's words if the cap doesn't fit, but we can certainly be open to what they have to say.

If the person says, 'I don't like what you did in that situation,' we could respond with, 'Thanks, I didn't realise this until you spoke to me.' With this level of openness, we welcome change and new possibilities and the result is continuous improvement. Accepting criticism is a necessary step to attaining excellence in anything we do. Criticism does not need to be seen as negative; it is a window of opportunity.

Einstein once said, 'We cannot solve our problems from the same level of thinking that created them,' so we will have to move to a different level of awareness if we are to go beyond the awareness in which the anger arose. The immediate need is to reach a higher plane of awareness.

What does that higher plane of awareness mean? It means not allowing the mind to express itself based on reactions, impressions, prejudices or judgments. And how do we train our mind to be without them? That is the crux of the matter. We need to find a way to evaluate and find solutions. We need to accept the reality of the situation and work from there.

Complaining and blaming others are signs of non-acceptance. In one sense the blame game turns us into helpless victims, while in another sense it leads us to solicit agreement and sympathy through gossip, justifying why it is not our fault; we avoid looking at ourselves by pointing the finger elsewhere.

Another tendency is to suppress anger, leading to a pressure cooker of emotion building up inside. Eventually the energy will implode within us or go cold and stagnate, leading to an undercurrent of resentment and bitterness. It will have its own consequences and will surely express itself in both mental and physical health issues.

What is a healthy response to the energy of anger? Let's visit the idea of acceptance. Take a scenario where someone has done something really bad to hurt your whole family. Does accepting the situation mean doing nothing? No. Someone once asked me, 'When does acceptance become irresponsible?' Acceptance doesn't mean being weak and cowardly. It only means accepting the reality of the present circumstances without reacting strongly in the moment. We move forward from there. Somehow a newer consciousness will open up and the right action will follow.

Heartfulness supports this in many ways, including:

Connecting with our Centre, which immediately creates balanced perception in us.

The Heartfulness Cleaning practice, which removes emotional complexities and helps us to let go of the strong emotional charge.

Transmission,[1] which can be a miraculous catalyst to manage anger, fear and stress.

## Awareness and attitude

Ask yourself, 'When I am angry, am I alert and aware of what is happening inside me or am I simply reacting from subconscious patterns?' Often it is the absence of awareness that triggers a reactive angry response. Through meditation, we learn to expand our awareness, so we are better able to manage anger.

When you are angry, notice how anger is flowing as energy through your system. Don't repress it, let it be there, become aware. This very act of witnessing shines a light in the darkness. When you become aware of what is happening inside you, it is easier for peace to descend. The energy that fueled the anger will now fuel peace, the quality of which you will have never experienced before. This contradiction

[1] Transmission is the specialty of Heartfulness Meditation, and it removes the inner complexities in our energy field, cleaning and illuminating the spiritual centres or chakras. Transmission removes the obstacles on our journey to the Centre. It makes meditation truly dynamic. You can read more about Transmission in the last chapter of the book.

is due to the nature of anger itself. As you become more and more aware, the time gap between your anger and its U-turn becomes less and less and as the gap continues to lessen with greater awareness, eventually it will tend toward zero and you will generally be at peace.

Awareness will also prevent us from suppressing anger, which happens when we are not able to process it or express it in a meaningful way. It builds up inside, leading to all sorts of mental, emotional and physical health issues, including depression and poor life satisfaction[2], negative emotions and feelings of inauthenticity[3], greater sympathetic activation of the cardiovascular system[4], conflict avoidance, guilt and rumination[5]. In addition, those who suppress anger also have a greater perception of lacking support[6]. The stimulation of the amygdala in the midbrain also increases aggression[7], especially passive aggression. In fact, the amygdala is key to processing aggressive information in

---

[2] Gross, J.J. & O.P., 2003. Individual differences in two emotion regulation processes: implications for affect, relationships, and well-being. *J Pers Soc Psychol* 85(2): 348-362.

[3] Ibid.

[4] Gross, J.J., 1998. Antecedent and response focused emotion regulation: divergent consequences for experience, expression, and physiology. *J Pers Soc Psychol* 74(1): 224-237.

[5] Kopper, B.A. & D.L. Epperson, 1996. The experience and expression of anger: Relationships with gender, gender role socialization, depression, and mental health functioning. *Journal of Counseling Psychology* 43(2): 158–165.

Martin, R.C. & E.R. Dahlen, 2007. Anger response styles and reaction to provocation. *Personality and Individual Differences* 43(8): 2083–2094.

[6] Palfai, TP. & K.E. Hart, 1997. Anger coping styles and perceived social support. *J Soc Psychol* 137(1): 105-111.

[7] Vaernet K. & A. Madsen, 1970. Stereotaxic amygdalotomy and basofrontal tractotomy in psychotics with aggressive behaviour. *J Neurol Neurosurg Psychiatry* 33(6): 858–863.

Vohs, K.D. et al., 2011. Ego depletion is not just fatigue: Evidence from a total sleep deprivation experiment. *Social Psychological and Personality Science* 2(2): 166-173

all of us. The midbrain is primed to produce this response in situations of threat or danger, so it all depends on how we perceive the world around us and what our subconscious mind thinks is dangerous.

Research on war veterans demonstrates that veterans with aggressive behavioral disorders have a more intense brain response to external stimuli, including the response from the amygdala. They also have lower connectivity between the amygdala and the prefrontal cortex of the brain[8]. This is because of the circumstances they lived through during wartime and the hypersensitivity they developed in their awareness of threats.

Finally, there is evidence to suggest that the suppression of emotions may result in the risk of an earlier death, including death from cancer[9].

How do we prevent all this? We start by being aware and then learning to master our responses from the inside. Inner peace dissolves the impulses of violence. It is in a peaceful environment that creativity finds true meaning. It is in a peaceful environment that mothers are able to nurture their children. It is in a peaceful environment that we witness and enjoy happiness and so many other wonderful things.

---

[8] Heesink, L. et al., 2018. Neural activity during the viewing of emotional pictures in veterans with pathological anger and aggression. *Eur Psychiatry* 47: 1-8.

Varkevisser, T. et al., 2017. Resting-state functional connectivity in combat veterans suffering from impulsive aggression. *Soc Cogn Affect Neurosci* 12(12): 1881-1889.

[9] Chapman, B.P. et al., 2013. Emotion suppression and mortality risk over a 12-year follow-up. *J Psychosom Res* 75(4): 381-385. doi:10.1016/j.jpsychores.2013.07.014.

Practising meditation develops our ability to be aware and present, so we reduce the time gap between anger and its U-turn. We respond faster with empathy and serenity.

Ask yourself another question: 'Why do I want to curb my anger?' Is it because you think it is sinful or because it creates stress and damages your system? If that is the case, your approach is a step higher than a person who gets angry all the time, but it arises out of the desire to prevent negative consequences rather than out of genuine compassion. It is the attitude with which you curb anger that will change your future. Is it so as not to injure another person or is it to protect yourself? It is better to opt for kindness and compassion.

## Learn to pause

When you are in a state of anger, you won't always think clearly and you won't respond with true kindness and empathy toward others, especially the person who triggered the anger in you. I have learned through experience that it is always good to take time out. Otherwise, if you do erupt in anger, its effect on others can be long-lasting and stressful, causing unnecessary damage.

If you observe yourself, you will find that you can't hold on to such explosive energy for more than 24 hours. By then it will have dissipated from your system or been internalised.

Regular meditation practice trains you to pause, reflect and postpone the reaction so that you may:

Feel some tenderness for the other person, as you come to appreciate their perspective.

Think, 'Thank goodness I didn't react.'

Realise that there is some truth in the other person's words. Then you can thank them for sharing their observations. Even when the other person is wrong, by not reacting you will preserve the relationship and improve the situation.

## Uncover your true nature

Emotions signal a vibrational change in your energy field – your field of consciousness. Often it is a subconscious, pre-programmed reaction from deep within the psyche, rather than something you have analysed or thought through. The thinking comes later. Once the vibrational shift happens, once the anger is activated, that energy needs to be used, otherwise it remains trapped until it finds closure. Similarly, a sad encounter with another person remains as an emotional imprint until it finds closure and love lost creates a vacuum. All these will have a ripple effect, both within you as well as on the other people in your life. Positive emotions also create energy fields. They result in an upward curve while the negative emotional memories result in a downward curve.

Those wise people who have mastered anger don't need to practise pausing, because they know how to use anger constructively in the first place. They anticipate situations and adjust themselves. Eventually, their inner state is of such a high order that there is no need for any adjustment. They recognise anger as a tool for transformation. The opposite extreme is seen in people who blame others and are not able to manage their anger, even when they realise the consequences of lashing out. Most of us are somewhere in between. We realise either during or after an angry outburst and try to adjust.

Wise people also learn how to master another sort of time gap – the gap between two distracting desires. We also want this duration to lengthen. As it does, so does the gap between two associated thoughts. Eventually it leads to a self-contained mind without the pulls and pushes of desires, emotions and thoughts: the peace of pure awareness.

This leads to another capacity, concentration – to fix our attention on one thing at a time. We can then move toward our most cherished goals in life. Inner peace dispels desires and ego and focussed attention takes us where we are headed. Together they allow us to move toward our highest potential. Our thoughts, ideas and intentions are slowly transformed and as the gap between each thought lengthens, there is space for feelings to surface; we start to experience feelings of various types.

## Feelings versus emotions

Let me distinguish here between feelings and emotions. Feelings are pure; emotions are filtered by our subconscious patterns. It's like lighting a fire – when the wood is dry and cured it will burn clear, without smoke, whereas when it is damp there will be smoke due to impurities. Feelings are simple and pure because they are not complicated by subconscious patterns. Emotions have layers of complexity. Our emotions therefore point us to whatever complexities we are carrying and show us what needs to go if we are to change and evolve in our subconscious patterns and tendencies.

Just as the gap between each thought lengthens, so eventually the gap between each feeling also lengthens, creating space for the idea of becoming to take hold. Then, the gap between each state of becoming also lengthens and on it goes ...

During meditation, as the gap between two thoughts lengthens, focused attention is the result. When the two thoughts are identical, it creates focused thinking. Likewise, when the gap between two feelings lengthens, their identical recurrence leads to focused feeling. And focused feeling brings emotional stability and peace.

We can compare this with a more changeable mental state. Try to remember the last time you were angry – how long did the anger last? What feelings followed immediately afterward and then later? What about a time when you were very happy and joyous? How long did that last and what followed? Sadness is followed by happiness, pleasure is followed by guilt, anger is followed by compassion and peace is followed by restlessness. There is constant change within, like the ever-changing formations of clouds in the sky. Our sky of consciousness keeps changing, based on our thoughts, feelings and conditions.

You can think and feel so many things in such a short period of time. In the morning, you may be restless and anxious due to an exam, whereas later, having done well, you are happy and relaxed. When your focus, your feelings and your condition keep changing, as well as your surroundings, you become vulnerable. Imagine a bird flying very fast – it is so difficult to photograph. Similarly, it is hard to pinpoint a mind that is constantly moving from one thought to another, one emotion to another, one feeling to another. And in the case of the mind, it moves faster than the speed of light! Can a wandering mind attain happiness?

The solution is to develop a focused mind. And that is only possible by doing some sort of mental practice, like the Heartfulness practices.[10] Single-pointed attention of the mind happens simply and effortlessly when we adopt these practices. The natural outcome of having a focused mind is that the heart remains steady. We remain constantly in tune with our feelings. If we also refine our outer behavior, we reach a level where single-pointedness of thought, feeling and condition become a steady state.

How does steadiness arise in meditation? Sometimes meditation is frustrating, because the mind is full of thoughts and emotions. We try to feel peaceful and still, but instead we are acutely aware of the activity within us. This is quite normal, especially at first. It is rare that we have single-pointed attention from the beginning. Concentration is the *result* of meditation, not the other way around. In Heartfulness, Transmission gives us glimpses of the focused state from the beginning and this provides an incentive to continue.

[10] Heartfulness starts with four basic practices: Relaxation, Meditation with yogic Transmission, Cleaning and Prayer. These practices complement one another. To learn more about them, visit www.heartfulness.org.

Eventually, we go beyond feeling to the state known as 'becoming.' In the time gap between two 'becomings' we are constant and still. As the time gap between two 'becomings' lengthens, the settled state paves the way for jumping into the abyss of the great unknown. Without steadiness of heart and mind, it is not possible.

A fluctuating changeable mind is a common state and the changeable nature of thoughts and feelings can eventually culminate in multiple personality disorders. An ever-changing mind and an ever-changing heart result in an ever-changing consciousness – many personalities in one person.

In all this, the middle factor of 'feeling' plays a major role. Constancy in feelings, the largest possible time gap between two feelings, is what defines a person.

## Why do we react the way we do?

In a sense, feelings and emotions are ours, but they can be triggered from outside as automatic reactions to situations. In fact, when the mind is not guided by the heart, it is easily affected from outside. Awareness, on the other hand, is beyond the mind and it is not controlled by external factors. So far, there is no scientific experiment that pinpoints a centre in the brain corresponding to awareness. The whole purpose of meditation and spirituality is to bring awareness of all that is the mind and to let go of our identification with it – to bring awareness, alertness and higher consciousness.

Understanding the mind through meditation gives us deep insight about what hurts us and why we react the way we do.

It all depends on our identification. If we identify with our body, any attack or criticism at the physical level will hurt, for example, 'Your face looks awful.' Most people are more insulted when their mind is attacked – 'Why don't you think!' – because we identify more deeply with the mind than the body. That is why bipolar disorder has more stigma attached to it than hypertension, even though both are serious diseases – one of is of the mind and the other of the body.

When someone attacks our intelligence, it is even more hurtful: 'How could you be so stupid!' And if someone attacks our ego, it hurts even more. The ultimate hurt comes when they attack our heart: 'You don't care about us,' or 'You don't know how to love.' From that perspective, the mind is more of an outside agency. When someone insults you and you become angry, the person's insult is the remote trigger. So how to be immune to such triggers?

If your mind is reacting to remote triggers, it is behaving like a gramophone record, according to the cognates of your past experience that have been laid down as neural pathways in the brain. As you go on removing the layers of identification, you will discover the awareness of your inner being, your soul. The realisation of that distinction between the mental cognates and the higher awareness of your soul is one of the greatest things that can happen to you, because then you are free!

When your mind is pretending to play the role of the master, instead of simply an instrument, you are a slave of your wishes, functioning like a puppet. This is where establishing a higher goal can help so much. When you focus on that goal, you naturally ignore any thoughts and feelings that distract you from it. Your whole life takes on a new dimension.

## Interacting with others

But anger is not only about us. What happens when others get angry? Do you try to correct them? Buying time is the best support you can give, as the anger will dissipate. If that is not possible, sit prayerfully, centre yourself and let the person discharge their explosiveness by listening deeply.

Make a silent subtle suggestion that their anger is being pulled out and that they are becoming more loving and understanding.

Can cheerfulness and anger go together? Just as fire doesn't emit coolness, anger doesn't emit and receive cheerfulness and love. So, even if you are healthy, wealthy and intellectually sound, what will happen if your ability to love and be loved is compromised? You can see the consequences.

Within you are all kinds of gifts – joy, humility, simplicity, purity, kindness and compassion and very strong moral muscles. If anger is misused, all these can be incinerated by one tiny spark. The fire of anger can destroy everything in its trail – physical health, individual peace, mental well-being, harmony in the family, mutual trust and the bridge connecting you with your higher consciousness. You may have a zillion justifications for lashing out, but why entertain them?

When you feel overwhelmed by anger, try the following tips:

- Sleep on the ground,
- Regularly do the Heartfulness Cleaning to remove it and
- Meditate upon the light blue colour.

I am reminded of a funny story. One morning, the Mulla Nasruddin was having tea at his favourite tea shop. A twelve-year-old boy came running through the door, went directly to the Mulla and knocked his cap off his head. The boy ran away, thinking this was a great joke and the Mulla picked up his cap and put it back on his head. For the next few days the same thing happened and the Mulla remained calm and unaffected, even though others in the tea shop were irritated by the boy's pranks.

One day, a friend asked the Mulla, 'Why don't you do something to teach that naughty boy a lesson? Don't you get angry?'
'It is useless,' the Mulla replied.
The very next day the Mulla arrived at the tea shop a little late and when he entered there was a soldier sitting at his usual table. So, he sat at another table. The boy entered like clockwork, following his daily routine and ran straight to the Mulla's regular table, knocking the cap off the soldier's head. The soldier got angry, caught the boy and lifted him off the ground, threatening all sorts of punishments.
Mulla Nasruddin turned to his friend and said, 'Now do you understand?'

## Anger as energy

Let's go back to the idea that anger is energy that cannot be destroyed and its higher purpose is to bring about personal improvement and change.

Whenever you are angry, become aware of the energy flow. Ask yourself, 'What is it telling me? What longings of mine are not being addressed? What can I do differently?' Use the opportunity to improve yourself. In such awareness there will be no aggression, only hope for a brighter future.

## Suggestions

Anger is energy. Notice how the energy of anger is flowing through your system. Don't repress it, let it be there, and become aware of your patterns, your needs and longings, and your reactions. Then ask yourself, 'What will I do differently?' Use the energy for purposeful change.

Every emotion signals a change of vibration in your energy field. Often it is a subconscious pre-programmed reaction that surfaces. Thinking comes later. See if you can wait till the reaction passes so that thinking is possible, and then reflect on what could change.

When you experience excessive anger:

- sleep on the ground,
- regularly do the Heartfulness Meditation and Cleaning and
- meditate upon the light blue colour.

Let go of expectations. Welcome criticism and challenges. Shift your awareness to look at the reasons for the anger from a different perspective. Meditation will help you to be aware, pause, and respond with wisdom.

When someone else is angry, silently suggest that their anger is being pulled out and they are becoming more loving and understanding.

# Cultivating Boundless Love and Compassion

MATTHIEU RICARD

## About Matthieu Ricard

Born in France in 1946, Matthieu is a Buddhist monk, author, translator, and photographer. He first visited India in 1967 where he met spiritual masters from Tibet. After completing his Ph.D. in cell genetics in 1972, he moved to the Himalayan region where he has been living for the past 45 years.

He is an international best-selling author and a prominent speaker on the world stage, celebrated at the World Economic Forum at Davos, forums at the United Nations, and at TED where his talks on happiness and altruism have been viewed by over seven million people. He is a charismatic figure who has captured the minds and hearts of people all over the world.

## A Buddhist perspective

Let me start with a true story. One of the Dalai Lama's doctors, Dr. Tenzin Chödrak, spent twenty-five years in communist Chinese forced labour camps. He had no sympathy for his torturers, but he didn't give in to hate. After the torture sessions, he was almost always able to regain his compassion for all sentient beings, including his torturers. He considered them as people who had been brainwashed, and who deserved his compassion not his hate. He said that he would not have been able to survive many years in such horrendous conditions if his heart had been constantly filled with animosity and resentment. Love and compassion gave meaning to his life.

As the Buddha Shakyamuni said, 'If hate replies to hate, hate will never cease.' Another great Buddhist master from the seventh century, Shantideva, wrote,

> No evil is there similar to anger,
> No austerity to be compared with patience.
> Steep yourself, therefore, in patience.
> In all ways, urgently, with zeal.[11]

---

[11] Shantideva, 2006. *The Way of the Bodhisattva* (Revised edition; Padmakara Translation Group, trans.). Boston: Shambhala.

Patience is rooted not in a feeble, passive resignation, but in a strong, courageous love and inner freedom. A much-loved Tibetan master from the nineteenth century, Patrul Rinpoche wrote,

> Overcome your enemy, hatred, with the weapon of love;
>
> Protect your family, the beings of the six realms, with the skillful means of compassion.[12]

The power of love to conquer aggression is illustrated by Buddha Shakyamuni's encounter with Mara, the personification of evil, which symbolizes ego-attachment. On the eve of his enlightenment, as the Buddha sat under the bodhi tree, the demon hosts of Mara's armies surrounded him like a huge black cloud. Raging with malice and envy, they shouted insults and hurled weapons, but the Buddha remained serene and filled with such loving kindness that their insults turned into beautiful melodies and their vicious missiles became a rain of flowers. With loving kindness, you will always vanquish malevolence; having to face hostility and aggression will only enhance your awakening consciousness.

Love and hatred may follow one after the other, but not at the same time. We can either extend our hand in friendship or give a blow with our fist – we cannot do both at the same

[12] See Patrul Rinpoche's biography, *The Enlightened Vagabond*, 2018, translated from Tibetan by M. Ricard, Shambhala Publications. The verses come from Dilgo Khyentse Rinpoche, 1993. *The Heart Treasure of the Enlightened Ones: The Practice of View, Meditation, and Action*. Shambhala Publications.

time. The more we bring thoughts of love, the less space there is for hatred in our mental landscape. As we keep generating thoughts of love, hatred becomes rare and weak, and eventually evaporates altogether.

Constructive states like love, compassion, and inner freedom, need to be cultivated. Conversely, negative states like hate, pride, jealousy, and craving need not be encouraged. Another of my masters, Jigme Khyentse Rinpoche, says, 'We don't have to train our mind to achieve frustration. We don't need a booster for anger or an amplifier for pride and vanity.' By contrast, even if we have a natural potential for love and compassion, they can be greatly enhanced through training our minds until they become second nature. In fact, they are in harmony with the 'primordial goodness' that is at the very heart of our heart and mind, which can be variously called the 'fundamental nature of mind,' 'mind in its true nature,' 'buddha nature,' 'pure awareness,' or 'primordial simplicity.'

Patrul Rinpoche goes on to say,

> *Don't follow after the object of hatred, look at the angry mind.*
>
> *Anger, liberated by itself as it arises, is the luminous emptiness.*

When we feel hatred toward someone, this hatred exists in our mind. As we becomes fixated on the thoughts or animosity, full-blown hatred develops. Hatred might seem extremely powerful, but where does it get the power to overwhelm us so easily? Is it some external force, a warlord with weapons? Where is it? Can we find it in our brain, our heart or anywhere else? Does it have any shape or colour? Does it burn like fire or crush like a boulder rolling down the hill?

Clouds may be utterly insubstantial, but they can darken the sky and obscure the sun. So, afflictive thoughts like hatred can obscure the pristine radiance of awareness. If we recognise the nature of pure awareness, hatred loses all its power to harm.

What we perceive as evil qualities in others often do not intrinsically belong to them: they are mostly super impositions of our mental constructs. If we can overcome the hatred within our own mind, all outer enemies vanish at once. It is said that it is easier to cover the soles of our own feet with leather than to try to cover the whole Earth with leather to protect our feet from thorns.

'No matter who it is you meet, know that they have already walked several times through hell,' writes French poet Christian Bobin. When a person's mind has already been inflamed by hatred, to have compassion means to view them the way a doctor would approach a patient who is mentally ill. First, we need to prevent harm. But, like a doctor who is able to address the source of mental illness without turning the patient's brain to pulp, we must consider all possible means of solving this problem without also falling victim to violence and hatred. If hatred answers hatred, the problem will never end. The time has come to apply the balm of compassion to our wounds, our pain, and the madness of the world.

It is said that one moment of anger can destroy years of patience. Although I am full of imperfections, anger is not my main obstacle (I have others!), and I can't remember ever getting very angry in the last twenty years. Yet, many years ago, in Nepal, a person came to the monastery where I lived who made my blood boil! They had swindled the monastery of a large sum of money, and had come by to lecture me on morality, advising me to be 'detached of all worldly matters.' My voice trembling with irritation, I told them to get lost and ushered them out the door. At the time, I was convinced my anger was perfectly justified. It was moments later that I came to see how destructive and stupid anger can be, reducing our clarity and inner peace and turning us into veritable puppets.

## Where does anger come from?

If we carefully observe ourselves, we see that the experience of anger is like having a high fever. It is a temporary condition, and we do not have to identify with it. When we look at anger in this manner, it evaporates under our gaze, like white frost under the morning sun.

Where does anger come from, how does it evolve, where does it disappear to? All we can say for sure is that it is born in the mind, lingers there a moment or two, and then dissolves there, like waves arising from the ocean and dissolving back into it.

This is what my root spiritual master Dilgo Khyentse Rinpoche said on this matter: 'This is what is called the natural liberation from anger at the moment it arises, by recognising its lack of inherent existence. This liberation happens spontaneously, like a sketch drawn on the surface of water.'

We should never underestimate the power of the mind to create and crystallise worlds of hatred, greed, jealousy or arrogance. Hatred exaggerates the faults of its object and ignores its good qualities. As psychologist Aaron Beck notes, 'Biased perceptions and thinking become set in a mental vise in response to threat, real or imaginary. This rigid frame, the prison of the mind, is responsible for much of the hate and violence that plague us.[13]'

When the mind is steeped in animosity and resentment, it encloses itself in delusion and is convinced that the source of its dissatisfaction is exterior to itself. Our perception of being wronged or threatened leads us to focus exclusively on the negative aspects of a person or a group. We fail to see people and events in the context of a much vaster web of interrelated causes and conditions. Forming the image of the 'enemy' as despicable, we generalise it to the whole person or the entire group. We solidify the 'evil' or 'disgusting' attributes we see in them as being permanent and intrinsic traits, and we turn away from any re-evaluation of the situation. By doing so, we obscure the basic goodness that allows us to appreciate everyone's aspiration to avoid suffering and achieve happiness.

Hatred is not expressed solely through anger, but the latter erupts the moment circumstances permit. It is linked to

---

[13] Beck, A., 1999. *Prisoners of Hate: The Cognitive Basis of Anger, Hostility, and Violence*, HarperCollins.

other negative emotions and attitudes: aggression, resentment, bitterness, intolerance, slander, and above all, ignorance. It can also stem from fear when we or those we love are threatened.

We also can learn to identify 'everyday' hatred connected to our immediate circle. What can we do when we hate our brother, our colleague or our ex-spouse? They obsess us. We brood over their faces, their habits, and their quirks until they make us sick; our obsession relentlessly converts mundane aversion into persecution.

Hatred is clearly corrosive, whatever the intensity and circumstances behind it. Once hatred has overwhelmed us, we are no longer masters of ourselves and are incapable of love and compassion. And yet hatred always begins with a few thoughts ...

As Mahatma Gandhi said, 'If we practise an eye for an eye and a tooth for a tooth, soon the whole world will be blind and toothless.' Rather than applying the law of retaliation, wouldn't it be better to relieve your mind of the resentment that is corroding it? Even if such about-faces are rare (only one of the indictees at Nuremberg, Albert Speer, regretted his actions), there's no reason not to hope for them.

A few months before she died at Auschwitz, Etty Hillesum wrote, 'I can see no way around it. Each of us must look inside himself and excise and destroy everything he finds there which he believes should be excised and destroyed in others. We may be quite certain that the least iota of hatred that we bring into the world will make it even more inhospitable to us than it already is.[14]'

## Practise love and compassion

To cultivate altruistic love and compassion, the mind must be ready, clear, and focused. To that end, start by improving your power of concentration, by concentrating your attention upon the in-and-out of your own breath, observing the sensation created by the passage of air through the nostrils when breathing in and out. All training involves effort, and all change encounters resistance. You can learn to overcome the obstacles to meditation, including mental agitation and its opposites, laxity and lethargy, as well as lack of perseverance. It is advisable to meditate regularly for multiple short periods rather than engaging from time to time in long sessions.

To meditate on altruistic love, begin by realising that deep down we all want to avoid suffering and aspire for happiness. This step is especially important if you have a negative image of yourself and have suffered a lot; if you think you are not meant to be happy. Once you have recognised this aspiration, it is easy to realise that it is shared by all beings without exception: none of them wants to suffer. This awareness will help you to feel closer to all beings, to value them, to be concerned about their fate, and to wish them well.

[14] Hillesum, E., 1983. *An Interrupted Life: The Diaries, 1941–43*. Translated by Arnold J. Pomerans. Jonathan Cape Ltd.

It is easier to begin the training in altruistic love by thinking about someone dear to you. Imagine a smiling child coming to you and looking at you happily, trustingly, full of innocence. Take the child in your arms and feel unconditional love and kindness. Be completely filled with this love, which wants nothing but the happiness of this child.

Then, extend those loving thoughts to people you know less well, and to strangers. They too want to be happy, even if they are sometimes clumsy in their attempts to escape suffering. Let's go further; include in this loving kindness those who have harmed you, and those who are harming humanity in general. Look at them the way a doctor looks at his most seriously ill patients. Finally, embrace all sentient beings in a feeling of limitless love.

## Practise unconditional compassion

Compassion is the form that altruistic love takes when it is confronted with the suffering of others. For this, you will feel concerned by the situations of others, realise their suffering, wish for them to be relieved from suffering, and be eager to act toward that aim.

Like before, first generate an unconditional compassion to someone dear to you who is enduring great suffering. Visualise every atom of that person being replaced by an atom of love. Then, extend this warm, loving compassion to all beings, forming a wish from the bottom of your heart: 'May all beings be freed from suffering and the causes of their suffering.'

Your compassion and love often reflect the benevolent or aggressive attitude of others toward you and your loved ones. You may find it difficult to extend compassion to bloody dictators and all those who do great harm to humanity at large and to all sentient beings. There is no question of condoning their behaviour and minimising the horrors they have perpetrated. Yet, compassion is not based on moral judgments; it aims at remedying all causes of suffering, whatever they are and whatever form they take. So, you can wish: 'May the hatred, cruelty, greed or cold indifference that drive them to harm others be cleared from their mind.'

## Practise rejoicing in virtue

There are beings in this world who possess rare qualities, others who benefit humanity greatly and are crowned with success, and others who, simply, are more talented, happier or more successful than we are. Can you fully and sincerely rejoice in their accomplishments, and wish that their qualities persist and increase? This ability to celebrate the good qualities of others is an antidote to envy and jealousy, feelings which reflect an inability to be happy at others' happiness. It is also a remedy for discouragement and a gloomy, despairing view of the world.

## Practise impartiality

Impartiality is an essential complement to the three previous meditations. The wish that all beings are free from suffering must be universal; it cannot depend on preferences or how others treat us. Love and compassion are like the sun that shines on all sentient beings, no matter who they are. It is true that some beings are closer to you, like your children, your parents, and other dear ones. They are like those who are closer to the sun due to the circumstances of this life; they will naturally get more light and warmth. But that is never at the cost of discriminating against others. The sun continues to shine on all beings. If you limit the sun of love and compassion so that it shines only on a few select people, it will not only cease to light and warm all others, but it will shine poorly even on your dear ones. Your altruism will shrink and be depreciated.

## Interweaving these four practices

When you meditate on altruistic love, you may stray into attachment with those people you are close to. When this happens, it is time to shift to meditating on impartiality, so as to extend this love to everyone – friends, strangers, and enemies.

Impartiality may then drift into indifference; instead of being concerned for all beings, you will feel distant from them, and stop being concerned by their fate. That is the time to shift to thinking of all the sufferings endured by the countless sentient beings throughout the world and to generate infinite compassion.

By meditating on the sufferings afflicting others, you may become overwhelmed by a sense of powerlessness in the face of the immensity of the task. Then, shift to rejoicing for all who manifest great qualities and accomplish admirable deeds for the benefit of others.

If this joy veers into naïve euphoria, return to meditating on altruistic love. And so on.

At the end of the session, return for a moment to your vision of the world. Contemplate again upon the interdependence of all things, and try to cultivate a fairer, less egocentric perception of reality. Understand that everything is impermanent, interdependent, and thus devoid of the autonomous existence you usually attribute to them. This realisation will lead to a freer way of perceiving the world. Try to remain for a few minutes in full awareness of the present moment, in a state of natural simplicity, in which the mind is free from discursive thoughts.

Before resuming your everyday activities, conclude with the intention to bridge meditation and daily life. To do so, sincerely dedicate the merit of having meditated to all sentient beings, thinking, 'May the positive energy created by this meditation and by all kind actions, words, and thoughts, past, present, and future, contribute to relieving the suffering of all beings, now and for all time to come.'

Love and compassion need not be restricted to your fellow human beings. It can be extended to the eight million other species that are our co-citizens in this world. It is estimated that just over 110 billion Homo sapiens have lived on Earth since our appearance on this planet. This is about the number of land and sea animals we kill every two months for our so-called 'needs.' If we wish to have a coherent ethic and altruistic love, we must extend the sense of justice and compassion to all sentient beings who experience suffering. As the French poet Lamartine said, 'A person doesn't have two hearts, one for animals and another for humans. One either has a heart or one doesn't.'

## Suggestions

Be patient. Don't give in to hate. Patience is a result of strength, courage, love, and inner freedom.

Love conquers aggression: The more loving thoughts you have, the less space there is for hatred.

Instead of following the object of your anger, look at your own mind. Overcome the hatred within, and outer enemies will vanish.

One moment of anger can destroy years of patience. Anger is like a high fever, it is temporary. Don't identify with it.

Four practices:

- Meditate regularly on altruistic love.
- Cultivate unconditional compassion.
- Rejoice in the accomplishments of others.
- Wish that all beings are filled with love and compassion and are free from suffering.

# An Evolutionary View of Anger and Love

JAMES DOTY

## About James Doty

James Doty M.D. is the founder and director of the Centre for Compassion and Altruism Research and Education (CCARE) at Stanford University of which His Holiness the Dalai Lama is the founding benefactor. He works with a variety of scientists from a number of disciplines examining the neural bases for compassion and altruism. Through CCARE, Dr. Doty has overseen the development of a variety of techniques, apps and programs to address issues of stress, anxiety and burnout.

He is also an adjunct professor in the Department of Neurosurgery at Stanford University School of Medicine. Dr. Doty is an inventor, entrepreneur, and philanthropist, having given support to charitable organisations supporting peace initiatives and providing healthcare throughout the world. He has supported research, provided scholarships, and endowed chairs at multiple universities.

Dr. Doty is on the boards of a number of non-profits,. is the former chairman of the Dalai Lama Foundation, and the former vice-chair of the Charter for Compassion. He is the Senior Editor of the *Oxford Handbook of Compassion Science* and is the author of the New York Times bestseller, *Into the Magic Shop: A Neurosurgeon's Quest to Discover the Mysteries of the Brain and the Secrets of the Heart*, which has now been translated into 40 languages and served as the basis for the third album, Love Yourself: Tear, of famous K-pop group, BTS. Dr. Doty's work has been cited in numerous media including *The Wall Street Journal*, *The New York Times*, *The Washington Post*, NBC, ABC, and many others.

# James Doty

## A neuroscientific perspective

All human beings have the sympathetic nervous system, which is one part of our autonomic nervous system (the other part being the parasympathetic nervous system). It is associated with the vagus nerve, which rises in the brainstem and is distributed to all the organs of the body, especially the heart. The vagus nerve provides a two-way communication, with signals coming from the organs to the brain, as well as from the brain to the organs. It is within this complex that the autonomic nervous system functions.

Anger is part of the sympathetic nervous system response, which allows us to fight or flee from danger. It is part of who we are. When we were on the savanna in Africa 16,000 years ago (remember that our DNA has not changed significantly in the last 200,000 years), events would have triggered the sympathetic nervous system. We would have fought potential predators or if something couldn't be overcome, we would have run away or pretended to be dead, in the hope that the predator would leave.

In our early evolution as a species, the sympathetic response was very helpful. The problem in modern society is that we are not on the savanna, and we are not in the context of a confrontation. So, many of us hold anger inside, and create a narrative of the event that triggered it, which is painted by the emotions we are feeling.

I would suggest that all of us, myself included, have to learn to deal with events that cause anger in us – whether it is someone not doing something we hoped they would do or someone we feel has hurt us – and how we respond to them. Anger is not dissipated; it is contained in memory, and every time we think of that memory it stimulates the same physiological response, which could be an increase in heart rate, an increase in blood pressure, and the release of hormones that affect our immune system and cause the release of protein. When we carry anger with us all the time, it essentially causes over-stimulation of the sympathetic nervous system, having a very deleterious effect on our overall health.

In fact, our systems were designed for a more natural environment. On the savanna in Africa, when anger was engaged people either succumbed or survived. When they survived, their system would immediately go back to the baseline state, but this doesn't happen to most of us in modern society. Instead, the negative emotion of anger, which is often associated with a perception of being wronged by somebody, creates a constant release of negative hormones, affecting us both mentally and physically.

## My journey

When I was younger, my background was challenging. I was surrounded by drugs and alcohol, poverty, and a mother with mental illness. I often felt angry, but I learned that anger never changed anything. It may have been useful on the savanna in Africa, but it was never helpful to me growing up. I had an immense amount of anger and hostility toward my parents, because I felt that I wasn't nurtured and loved. As a result, I carried anger with me and it had negative consequences.

In addition to the stimulation of the sympathetic nervous system, and all the negative effects I mentioned, it also doesn't allow you to be discerning and thoughtful, because the sympathetic system results in a fast response, not a calm thoughtful response. You are in survival mode, and therefore it is difficult to make thoughtful decisions about how to respond.

And when you carry anger and hostility, other people know your emotional state based on the way you speak, your facial expressions, your body language, and even your smell. They react to it. They approach you with caution, and it is hard to be your best self, because they are not sure how you are going to react. Being angry and hostile impairs your ability to be your best self.

If you have read my book, *Into the Magic Shop*, you will know that I carried hostility, anger, shame, despair, until I realised that my view of events was simply one view, tainted by what I felt I needed that was missing. After spending time with this woman, Ruth, who gave me insight, training in meditation, and the ability to look at the world in a different way, I realised that events are simply events. They have neither a positive nor a negative aspect to them. The positivity or negativity arises from within us. It is this creation of our own mental state that causes so much suffering.

Happiness is not a manifestation of our external environment, but a manifestation of our internal environment. Take the example of two people walking outside in a rainstorm: One person is in a suit and tie, running for an appointment without an umbrella, cursing, angry and upset at the fact that his suit is wet, and the rain has interfered with his day. The other person walks out into the same rainstorm and says, 'What a joy to be in the rain. It reminds me that I'm alive, the plants are being nourished, and I'm part of Nature. This is the most wonderful thing that has happened to me today.' Both people have experienced the exact same event.

I learned that anger did not help me to resolve any issues exterior to myself, neither did it help me with internal issues. Often it only made matters worse, because in anger you cannot see the true nature of reality.

I'll give you another example: One day, a person I have worked with for some time came into my office and was immediately aggressive and hostile. As per human nature, my sympathetic nervous system was stimulated. I could have responded by fighting – being aggressive back, retreating or playing dead – but instead I looked at this person and said, 'This is not how you usually are. What is really wrong, because it can't be the issue we are meeting about? Are you able to tell me what is wrong?' He burst into tears. Two days earlier, he found out that his wife had breast cancer. It turned out that his anger and aggressiveness toward me were out of fear and despair about what his future held. By approaching him in a different way, and not being angry myself, it allowed me to see clearly and offer support instead of anger.

Viktor Frankl, who wrote *Man's Search for Meaning*, has often been quoted as saying that between stimulus and response lies a pause and within that pause lies our freedom. I think this is the case with anger. When an event occurs, we have a choice about how we respond to that event. A person with self-awareness, who has spent time understanding their own angry reactions, who has life experience and insight, will not allow themselves to immediately succumb to the sympathetic nervous system's reaction to events. They know that being reactive will not lead to the best decision; it will not be discerning, it will not be thoughtful, and it will lead to the release of a whole lot of chemicals that aren't healthy.

So, what I try to do first in these situations is to be non-judgmental, because being judgmental is another thing that doesn't help. When we make assumptions about others, based on how they approach us, how they're dressed, on their educational level or their background, we are often wrong. Sometimes very wrong. So, I try to have a non-judgmental outlook, understanding that often when people approach us with negative emotion it actually has nothing to do with us or the present situation. It has to do with them. That negative emotion may have occurred at a different time and a different place, but they have not processed it or perhaps they don't have the tools to respond in an effective way.

So, having an evenness in temperament or equanimity prevents us from going to the extremes of our own emotional lability – not getting lost in anger, and also not getting lost in jubilation, because both can cloud our ability to see the true nature of reality. It is easy to attach emotionally to an event, not understanding that all these events are transitory, as are the emotions associated with them. It is easy to wish that those events which make us happy will persist, but it is this desire or attachment for such an outcome that causes us to suffer, because of our expectations.

## How I manage anger

Wisdom and understanding don't happen overnight for anyone. Often, the lessons we learn are a result of our own pain, suffering, and anger. We know the downside of things; certainly, that has been my experience. The woman in the magic shop helped me with many things, and one was to have more clarity, not clouded by emotion. I think that's a very important lesson.

I think the other aspect is my daily practice, which has evolved for me. When I wake up, I sit by the side of my bed, close my eyes, breathe in and out, with intentionality to relax. Then I think of the beauty of our existence, and I feel joy and awe about the world and my presence in it. Then, with intention, I go through an opening of the heart: I start with compassion for myself, and understand that I have my own suffering that can impair my decision making, and impair my ability to look at people in a non-judgmental way; I recognise the dignity in every person along with their suffering; I cultivate equanimity, and I practise forgiveness, because that's one of the greatest sources of anger – carrying the resentment that someone has harmed me.

The negative emotion may affect us without having any effect on the person we're angry with. It's like drinking poison and thinking it will hurt the other person. So, having forgiveness, having gratitude, having a set of values, integrity, understanding, a sense of fairness, practising kindness toward others with no motivation other than that, with no expectation of receiving anything, are all important. And unconditional love brings with it feelings of warmth and contentment.

Then I go out into my day in the world, referring back to the affirmation of the heart. It allows me to reset my intention throughout the day.

I think this is something that all of us can do: As soon as we feel angry or upset, step back for a moment, slowly breathe in and out, and get back to that state where we feel centreed, where we are not at the mercy of our emotions. Then we again understand that these things are transitory and oftentimes insignificant and meaningless.

As an example, my son came into the house the other day wearing his new tennis shoes. He had been running in the backyard and they were completely covered in mud. I was angry and upset at him, and I was about to start screaming at him, until I realised the reality that they're shoes, and they can be cleaned up, and he's a kid. So, we have to be careful about what we allow to stimulate us. In that instance, I had frustration about issues I had carried home from work. I transferred that emotion to my son, thinking he was the problem. He wasn't the problem; I was the problem.

## The effects of anger on health

We know that when we are chronically stressed, unhappy or angry, it has a profoundly negative effect on our health. As an example, when we have a chronic elevation of stress hormones like catecholamines, epinephrine and norepinephrine, it causes a decrease in heart rate variability. So, if a person with a heart rate of 60 is particularly stressed, the inter beat variability will be minimal, with one heartbeat every second. A relaxed person will have a more flexible inter beat variability, perhaps from 1.1 to 0.9 seconds, which is a healthy response. And we know that reduced heart rate variability is associated with the highest instance of sudden cardiac death.

We also know that people who are anxious, stressed or angry often have chronically elevated blood pressure, and this is associated with negative effects on the blood vessels, which can lead to a stroke. We know that a person who is often angry and frequently upset has a compromised immune system and an increase in inflammation in the body. This can increase susceptibility to the occurrence of infections. Chronic inflammation and a depressed immune response can also increase susceptibility to disease, and increase the severity of diseases like diabetes and heart disease. So, chronic anger, anxiousness, and fear have a hugely negative physiological consequence. Ultimately, they also have an effect on the length of the telomeres – the protective caps on our chromosomes. A decrease in telomere length is associated with a decrease in life expectancy.

So, carrying negative emotions, whether we are angry or upset, has an overall negative effect on well-being.

## Helping others to manage anger

During the evolution of our species, the stress response has proven to be very useful in many situations, and we certainly don't want to get rid of it. Yet as a species we have not learned to live in modern society without the chronic activation of our sympathetic nervous system. We do know that giving people insight and awareness of this reality, giving them tools to respond to the sympathetic response, like meditation, breathing exercises, and learning to pause before a response, can diminish their stress.

When we relax, breathe, and pause, we understand that other people are responding as a manifestation of their own mental state. Generally, they are not trying to be mean to us, they are just responding to events they are carrying with them. They may not have learned how to mitigate that. They may be suffering or hurt, as happened in the situation with the colleague I mentioned earlier. Many people who are hurting lash out at others. It is our choice how we respond to them. I think the best response is to ask, 'What is it that is causing you pain?'

When we teach these tools of relaxation to children, they learn. In a variety of studies where these techniques have been implemented, even in kindergarten, we see a decrease in bullying, a decrease in fidgeting, and an increase in attendance and academic performance. If we cannot regulate our emotions, we can't be attentive. To learn, we have to be present.

## Exploring love

We can look at love in many ways. First, it is the feeling we get when we are with someone who loves us back. It feels unconditional – we can tell them anything and we are not judged. This is necessary for us to expose our shadow self. What do many of us do with the shadow self, the part of us we find negative or disgusting? Push it away and pretend it is not a part of us. That only creates difficulty because it is not possible to do that. It *is* part of us. All of us have a shadow self. When we understand that, integrate it into ourselves, and still love and care for ourselves, we are at peace.

This is what happens with romantic love. A person unconditionally accepts us, with our good and our bad aspects; amazingly, they love us.

Another aspect is what we may perhaps call platonic love – understanding that every human being is worthy of love. And this is hard. It is easy to love our children and those who belong to our 'tribe,' because we identify with them. It is much more challenging to love people who have very different views to ours.

This is something we all need to work on – to expand our capacity to love in ever enlarging circles. When we develop the capacity to look out, and rather than seeing the other we see ourselves, I think that is the highest form of love. Then we include everyone and give them of ourselves, which is hopefully unconditional love. I believe this is the reality of transcendence because there is no longer separation.

## James Doty

### The effect of love on healing

When patients visit physicians, they are often anxious and scared. They may even be angry at the diagnosis they have received. This depresses their immune system, as well as leading to several other negative physiologic effects. We now know that when you lean toward them, when you touch them, when you make them feel that you are not rushing them, it has a profoundly positive effect on their physiology. Their heart rate decreases, their blood pressure decreases, and all the attributes that we have been talking about of giving love (in some sense that's what this is) are expressed. When you create that environment, the length of hospital stays decreases, wound healing improves, and a whole variety of other positive things occur. There is a study about people who are frequent repeat visitors to the emergency department of a hospital – people in poverty, some homeless, often with a variety of diseases. When simple kindness and love with intention were shown to them, their number of visits to the emergency department decreased by 50 per cent.

I tell my residents, 'Although we are in a very sophisticated field that has a lot of highly technical equipment, my successes as a physician and a neurosurgeon are as dependent on how I treat and care for the patients as the surgery itself.' And this reality has been demonstrated over and over again. In fact, people come to me in pain, but their pain has nothing to do with the imaging studies I'm looking at. It is a manifestation of their own psychic injury and damage, and the anger they carry. A physician who understands the importance of being kind, being caring, being embracing, being non-judgmental, has a very positive effect on their patients.

## Moderation

In some ways, it's like the oft repeated phrase, 'Everything in moderation.' Without some degree of stress we can't live. In fact, life would be quite boring. We need the difficult aspects of our journey to self-actualize, while understanding that extremes in both anger and love can be very deleterious. I am sure that excessive love has resulted in just as much pain as excessive anger.

When you are dependent, when you are attached, when you are wanting, it can make you blind, so that you don't see the true nature of reality. It is very similar to what happens when your anger gets out of control. Maintaining your equanimity is so important; so integrate that into your life. While the wonderful experience of being deeply in love with someone is extraordinary, and you want to hold on to it, living in that chronic state often blinds you to what is actually going on. So does constantly craving the feeling that someone loves you or needs you. It can be very negative at the end of the day. It is important to be able to accept that it is wonderful, but not be lost in it.

I think it is the same with negative events and anger. Anger serves a purpose – it makes you cautious, it makes you wary, it can be very helpful. But it's not helpful when it gets out of control, when you injure or kill someone. When you are able to temper and modulate it, and use it for a useful purpose, it can help you see things with clarity. You realise that anger can offer you an intense viewpoint of self-awareness, and it is then a learning experience. Again, it is having the evenness of temperament to embrace both, along with presence and unconditional love, so that the whole experience becomes extraordinary. Anger, pain, and suffering can give incredible insight.

More learning occurs in these negative states than in the positive ones, because in love you are in bliss, and you are not paying attention. When you are hurting or angry, it jars you and you gain insight. Being aware of the negative aspects of each experience, being able to view them with evenness of temperament, without getting lost in the extremes of emotion, will keep you centreed, and it will actually make you happy.

## The value of acceptance

From both the spiritual-religious and scientific perspectives, you have to accept people where they are at. What do I mean by that? Whether you use the framework of Maslow's hierarchy of needs or the context of karmic learning by living various lives, the reality is that there are some people who are not ready to be self-actualised during this lifetime; it is not their time to do so. Even those people who have gone beyond the level of seeking the basics like shelter, security, and food to a more social state, may not be ready for self-actualisation. We must learn to accept and respond to that as well. I believe that there is only a small percentage of people who have a yearning to see the larger idea, who understand that existence is transitory, and happiness does not come from self-absorption and narcissistic pursuits, but is the manifestation of serving others.

When we commit to this way of being in the world, and seeing the world in this way, then we are transcendent. The understanding is there that our purpose is ultimately reached in this world when we are being of service to others, and this requires us to be our best selves and reach our full potential.

## *Suggestions*

Anger is associated with a sympathetic nervous system response, known as the fight or flight response. It alerts us to danger and helps us survive. It only causes problems when it is out of control and coloured by other emotions. Cultivate clarity, so that your inner state is no longer clouded by emotions. When you are angry, you won't see the true nature of reality.

Observe yourself. Anger is evident in your speech, facial expressions, body language, etc., even when you try to suppress it.

Events are simply events. It is your mental state, your creation, that causes the suffering. Happiness is also a manifestation of your internal environment.

Practices:

- Breathe slowly, relax, centre yourself.
- Celebrate the beauty, joy, and awe of existence.
- Open your heart, develop self-compassion, feel the dignity and suffering of all beings.
- Cultivate equanimity, practise forgiveness.
- Have no expectations of receiving anything.
- When others are angry, ask them, 'What is causing you pain?'

# Learning to Master Anger

PIR ZIA INAYAT-KHAN

## About Pir Zia Inayat-Khan

Pir Zia carries the Sufi lineage of his grandfather, Hazrat Inayat Khan. He received his Ph.D. in Religion from Duke University. His books include *Saracen Chivalry: Counsels on Valor, Generosity, and the Mystical Quest*, *Mingled Waters: Sufism and the Mystical Unity of Religions*, and *Dream Flowers: The Collected Works of Noor Inayat Khan*. Pir Zia is president of the Inayatiyya and founder of the Suluk Academy. Now based in Richmond, Virginia, he and his family live both in the United States and France.

## A Sufi perspective

Hazrat 'Ali once overpowered an adversary on the battlefield and prepared for the final blow. At that decisive moment, the soldier spat in Hazrat 'Ali's face. Hazrat 'Ali paused, then threw down his sword and walked away. The soldier was dumbfounded. He pursued Hazrat 'Ali and pressed him for an explanation. Hazrat 'Ali answered, 'I am the Lion of God, not a lion of passion ... I am not a straw; I am a mountain of gentleness, patience, and justice.'

This story, told by Maulana Rumi in his *Masnavi*, illustrates the peace and dignity that comes by mastering anger. Anger is an intrinsic part of human life, but to fall under its power it is to become a creature of passion. One who controls anger is a master, and one who rises above it is a saint.

Anger is a symptom of frustrated desire. All beings are driven to obtain their ends, and when opposition intervenes anger often shows itself. Those who entertain few expectations are the least subject to anger, whereas those who expect the most are most prone to it. If Hazrat 'Ali's expectation of respectful treatment had exceeded his patience and humility, he certainly would not have thrown down his sword. But he was a mountain of gentleness, and therefore his name is revered to this day. He is respected for not demanding respect.

## Practices to manage anger in daily life

Imam Ghazali prescribes a number of treatments for anger:

When becoming angry, stop and reflect on the damage likely to be caused. Look back on the times you spoke or acted in anger. Did any good come of it? The consequences of a rash decision can last a lifetime. In fact, the effects of our actions extend beyond our mortal life.

Think that all that happens is divine decree, even if it is not to your liking. What has happened is what had to happen; there is no gainsaying destiny. Still, everything is changeable, and in fact it may be your personal destiny to meaningfully alter the course of events. But anger and the power to effect change are two different things.

Observe the expression on your face when you are angry. Stop and look in the mirror. Is this the face you wish to present to the world, the contorted face of a scowling ogre?

If you are standing, sit; if sitting, lie on the ground on your side. The Earth is humble and patient, and proximity to the Earth inculcates these qualities through a subtle osmosis. If the Earth does not bring you calm, Imam Ghazali recommends the use of cool water. When Hazrat 'Umar was angry, he sniffed water so that his wrath cooled.

Anger spreads like fire. You might be entirely at ease at one moment, and the next someone burning with rage comes along and provokes you. Now you, too, are burning. Why should that be? Why should someone else's agitation become yours? You may have no control over another's state, but your own state is fully in your keeping. Giving in to anger is a choice, though one that is usually made unconsciously.

Body and mind are linked through the current of the breath. When the breath is gentle and rhythmic, peace comes naturally to the body and mind alike. When the breath is disturbed, confused words and deeds follow; hence, the necessity of being well acquainted with the natural condition of your breath.

When the breath falls out of rhythm, you will immediately notice the slip and refrain from taking action until your breath returns to its natural state. Sayyid Abu Hashim Madani said, 'People say there are many sins and virtues, but I say there is only one sin: to let one breath go without being conscious of it.'

Anger is a sign that something needs attention. At such moments, to become overwhelmed by emotion is to miss the opportunity for reflection. If you are able to bring the heart to a state of clear awareness, wonderful openings become possible.

## A contemplative practice: The four dimensions of the heart

Hazrat Inayat Khan describes the heart's wisdom as having four aspects: perception, understanding, compassion, and the ideal. Perception is the length of the heart, understanding is its depth, compassion is its breadth, and the ideal is its height. When all four dimensions are awakened, sight becomes clear.

The four dimensions of the heart may be activated one after another as an unfolding contemplation:

> When anger is aroused, the first step is to notice the anger. Then, instead of lashing out, endeavor to rebalance the breath. When the breath is rhythmic, contemplation can begin.
>
> The contemplation begins with a survey of the situation before you. What are the facts on the ground? See things exactly as they are, shorn of projections born of hope or fear. That is perception.
>
> Next, turn to understanding and contemplate the roots of the situation. What are the underlying causes that have led to this moment? On reflection, you will realise that what is occurring has been long in the making.
>
> Then move to compassion. See how everyone struggles and suffers. No one's pain is separate from anyone else's.
>
> Finally, imagine the ideal. Conceive the greatest good that is possible in the situation: not merely what is best for yourself, but what is best for all. Seeing it clearly, you may resolve to work for it, unburdened by anger.

## Suggestions

Be a mountain of gentleness, patience, and justice.

Anger is a symptom of frustrated desire. Have fewer expectations if you wish to manage anger.

When you are angry, try to reflect on the damage you may cause and think that everything is coming from God. If you are standing, sit. If you are sitting, lie on the ground on your side, as the Earth will calm you. If that doesn't work, use cool water.

Practices:

- Perception: Notice the anger. Rebalance your breath by breathing gently and rhythmically. Don't do anything until your breath becomes natural.
- Contemplation: Survey the situation. What are the facts?
- Understanding: What are the underlying causes? Bring your heart to a state of clear awareness so that you can reflect on the cause of the anger.
- Compassion: Move to compassion. Acknowledge everyone struggles and suffering.
- The ideal: Conceive of the greatest possible good for all. Resolve to work for it.

# Recognising Our Wounds and Awakening to the Power of Love

LLEWELLYN VAUGHAN-LEE

## About Llewellyn Vaughan-Lee

Llewellyn Vaughan-Lee Ph.D. is a Sufi teacher and author. Born in London in 1953, he has followed the Naqshbandi Sufi path since he was nineteen. He has written a series of books giving a detailed exploration of the stages of spiritual and psychological transformation experienced on the Sufi path, with a particular focus on the use of dreamwork as inner guidance on the journey. Since 2000 the focus of his writing and teaching has been on the awakening global consciousness of oneness, and spiritual ecology, the need for a spiritual response to our present ecological crisis (see *Spiritual Ecology: The Cry of the Earth*). He has also been featured in the TV series Global Spirit and was interviewed by Oprah Winfrey as a part of her Super Soul Sunday series. His most recent book is *Seasons of the Sacred: Reconnecting to the Wisdom within Nature and the Soul.*

# Llewellyn Vaughan-Lee

## My story

I learned about anger at a young age. Love was something I only discovered much later. My mother was an angry person, with a cold piercing anger that could twist like a knife. Her anger destroyed her relationships, and when I was fourteen it destroyed our family. Like many children, I became only too familiar with anger, its cruelty, and the pain it caused both to the person who was hurt and also to my mother. I stayed with her when the family broke, and learned to live with her anger, the ways to avoid it, to defend against it.

Ours was not a generation that could talk to our parents, so I never learned the source of her anger, but I sensed it came from something broken within her at an early age. As with many people, her anger covered and protected a deeper, unacknowledged wound. I also discovered that she never knew love. Later I would remember that during my childhood I never heard the words 'I love you.' Love was simply not present in those early gray days.

It was later that I would experience love – the colour, the warmth, the light it would bring. I was nineteen when I met my teacher, an elderly Russian woman who had just come back from India, where she had been trained by a Sufi master.[15] In her little room beside the train tracks in North London, love was present. Not personal love – not the motherly warmth I never had or the tenderness of a lover's touch – but a simple, pure, unbounded, effortless power that seeped through all my defenses, through all my patterns of identification, my sense of self. The first love I knew was divine presence, that sweet wine that intoxicates everything it touches, making every cell in the body alive in joy and wonder. And it was effortless. It was a gift.

I remember coming home from a meditation meeting once, and saying to my mother, 'There was so much love.' She became angry, telling me that love was something to be worked for, that love was hard and difficult. But the love I knew was not. It was a gift. Only many years later did I come to understand that this love is a divine substance, the foundation of life, the primal song of creation. At the time I only knew that love was present, unasked for, unexpected, and that slowly this love, this sip of divine wine, worked its magic, and drew me back to God, whom the Sufis call 'the Beloved.[16]'

Love calls to us in many different ways. While most people seek for love in the tangle of human relationships, the mystic is drawn deeper under the surface – in Rumi's words, to 'return to the root of the root of your own being.' And

[15] The Russian woman who was my teacher was Irina Tweedie, who describes her spiritual training in the book *Daughter of Fire, A Diary of a Spiritual Training with a Sufi Master*. Her teacher, whom she refers to as Bhai Sahib, was Radha Mohan Lal.

[16] In Sufism the relationship with God is that of lover and Beloved. The Sufi wayfarer travels down this mystical path of love from the pain of longing, of being separate from God, to the bliss of merging, experiencing union with the Beloved within the heart.

here we discover one of life's greatest secrets: Love is at the source of all that exists. It *is* the source of all that exists.

Love is not just a feeling between people, but an energy, a divine spark that is present within everything. And it is this deepest essence – this substance of love – that we need to nourish us. This is what was awakened in me through the simple practice of sitting at the feet of my teacher and meditating on the heart.[17]

## Love flows through everything

Love speaks to our soul and to our body. Love includes all the senses – taste, touch, smell, sight, and sound. Love by its very nature includes everything. It can be found anywhere because it is everywhere. The mystic uncovers the simple secret: In truth love flows through everything – sweet, tender, aching, knowing, as well as dark and passionate. And as this primal energy, this greatest power, awakens within us, within our heart, our soul, it draws us deeper into its own mystery, into the secret of oneness, which Sufis call the unity of being.

My mother lived in the pain of her anger, and knew nothing of this love. Fractured by her own pain, she was always angry with someone else, unaware of this deeper oneness that is all around and within us. Anger may be justified, and sometimes it comes unbidden, triggered from the depths by

[17] See 'The Sufi Meditation of the Heart' by Llewellyn Vaughan-Lee, (https://goldensufi.org/articles_interviews.html)

some outer event or accusation. But anger is rarely an answer. It draws us apart, while love belongs to healing and wholeness. Love speaks to each of us reminding us that we *belong*, that we are all part of a living unity we call life, this great community, linked in visible and invisible ways. For the lover, it is a reminder that we belong to the Beloved.

## Working with the unconscious

On this journey toward wholeness, it is important to go beneath the surface, to recognise our wounds and pain. As Carl Jung wisely remarked, 'One does not become enlightened by imagining figures of light, but by making the darkness conscious. The later procedure, however, is disagreeable and therefore not popular.[18]' This inner work requires us to confront, accept, and finally transform the often unacknowledged roots of our anger and other negative feelings, so that we are no longer imprisoned by them or project their darkness onto others.[19] The Sufis call this 'polishing the mirror of heart,' so that the light of love can shine brightly, so that we can see clearly.

In the Sufi tradition I have followed[20] there are primarily two ways of working with anger. The first is the demanding psychological work of descending into the darkness of the psyche, where, through the light of consciousness and the power of love and acceptance, the raw anger or pain is

[18] Jung, C., 1968. The Philosophical Tree. *Collected Works 13: Alchemical Studies*, p. 335 Routledge, UK.

[19] This transformation of 'the shadow' is expressed simply in the saying, 'I looked and looked, and saw and saw, that what I thought was you and you is really me and me.'

transformed. This is the ancient alchemical work of turning lead – the primal energy of our psyche – into the gold of our true nature.

The second is by using the *dhikr* or mantra, the repetition of the name of God said inwardly with the breath. The dhikr is a powerful agent of transformation. Working in the unconscious it both realigns our psychic structure and transforms its energies. The dhikr is an archetypal sound and word symbol, which is magnetically aligned with the path, and acts as a transformer of psychic energy. The dhikr has the potential to arouse, concentrate, and transmute the energies of the unconscious. It disentangles and frees us from the knots and psychological blocks with which we have consciously and unconsciously enchained ourselves. How many difficulties I have resolved walking the streets of north London, silently repeating His name with all my inner concentration. The rhythm of my footsteps, the rhythm of my breath, and the light of my longing singing the divine name, all combined in the process of purification – this ancient work of polishing the heart.

My own path expanded to encompass love, from pain and defensiveness to joy and openness. At this moment, our world seems caught in so many divisions, and all the patterns of anger rooted in this divisiveness – religious, racial, ideological, social. There is always an 'other' to project our anger. There are so many different factions

[20] I belong to the Naqshbandi Sufi tradition, which has always had a strong psychological element. We are also known as the 'silent Sufis' because we practise the silent *dhikr* inwardly with the breath.

shouting their beliefs, distorted by social media and fake news. We are caught in the patterns of dualism, us against them, anger and its many voices ripping apart our world.

## Love is the language of unity

I often wonder if these voices of anger mask the unacknowledged pain of our culture's betrayal, the false promises of materialism, that having 'stuff' will make us happy. And the even deeper anguish of our collective soul, that we have 'broken the great conversation[21]' with the rivers and forests, the wind and the stars, that speaks to us of our real belonging, the interbeing of all life. We have lost our connection with the sacred nature of creation, its mystery and wonder, and as a result we feel wounded and lost. And around these feelings swirl the present dynamics of power and corruption, greed, and exploitation. This is a story of separation, of brokenness, of domination rather than cooperation.

And yet, love is what calls to us in our depths, even as the voices of anger scream louder. And the story of love is oneness, manifest in life's multihued unity, expressed in systems founded upon interrelationship and interdependence. We know how these patterns form the ecological basis of life. In past centuries we focused on the Darwinian model of struggle for survival, and the dynamics

[21] 'We are talking to ourselves. We are no longer talking to the rivers and forests, we are no longer listening to the winds and the stars. We have broken the great conversation. By breaking that conversation, we have shattered the universe. All the disasters that are happening now are a consequence of this spiritual autism.' Thomas Berry, *The Dream of the Earth*.

of competition that relate to that perspective. And life does have those forces of aggression, domination, and competition. But in recent years our understanding has shifted to recognise that 'the biosphere can be seen as a cooperative communal venture among all living organisms.[22]' The forest is not formed of individual trees competing for nutrients and sunshine, but is a single living organism connected by underground fungal networks forming cooperative interdependent relationships, maintained by communication and a collective intelligence similar to an insect colony.[23] This is the inherent reality of the natural world, which only works by the interdependent networks that connect each species in the web of life.

So how can we turn from the divisiveness of anger – its wounding and pain – to the unity of love, to cooperation rather than isolation? How can we change the story of separation to a story of living oneness?

When I was nineteen, I was given a simple practice of filling my heart with love. Half a century later, if I have learned anything, it is the power of love. And there are many ways to open the heart, many forms and expressions of love. There are simple acts of loving kindness toward friends and family, in the community or with strangers. These 'small things with great love,' are more potent and powerful than we realize, because they reconnect us with the spiritual roots of

[22] Lipton, B., 2010. The Biology of Inspiration, *Healing the Heart of the World*, Editor, Dawson Church, Elite Books, USA.

[23] See the works of Peter Wohlleben, for example, *The Hidden Life of Trees*, 2015, Ludwig Verlag, Germany.

life and its transformative and healing energies. Cooking a meal with love and care, listening to another's troubles with an open heart, touching your lover's body with tenderness or going deep in prayer until you merge in love's infinite ocean – in all these ways we live the love that unites us. And through our loving we nourish life in unseen ways. Because life is an expression of love, each act of love is a participation and gift to the whole.

At this time of ecological crisis – as we tear apart the fragile web of life – there is a vital need for us to love the Earth, to bring her into our hearts and prayers. We have a spiritual as well as a physical responsibility for 'our common home,' and she is calling out to us, crying for our help and healing. In the words of Thich Nhat Hanh:

> 'Real change will only happen when we fall in love with our planet. Only love can show us how to live in harmony with nature and with each other and save us from the devastating effects of environmental destruction and climate change.[24]'

We need to reawaken to the power of love in the world. It is our love for the Earth that will heal what we have desecrated, that will guide us through this increasingly toxic landscape and help us bring light back into our darkening world. Love links us all together in the most mysterious

[24] Hanh, T.N., 2013. *Love Letter to the Earth*, Parallax Press, USA, p. 29. In the same passage he writes, 'When we recognise the virtues and talents of the Earth, we feel connected to her and love is born in our hearts. We want to be connected. That is the meaning of love: to be at one.'

ways, and love can guide our hearts and hands. And the central note of love is oneness. Love speaks the language of unity rather than separation.

## The deepest secret of life

Love can open us to deep participation in the life of the whole; it can teach us to listen to life, feel life's heartbeat, sense its soul. It can awaken us to the sacred within all of creation, and it can reconnect us with what Indigenous Wisdom Keepers call the Original Instructions – how to live in harmony with the ecosystem, how to return to ways of praise and thanksgiving that honour and respect life's many forms, and the ways they support and nourish each other.

From this inner attitude we can begin to respond. When our hearts are open, we recognise that who we are and what we do affects the environment, both outer and inner. We learn to live in a more sustainable way, aware that real sustainability belongs to all of creation, not just 'greening the economy' that supports our present energy-intensive consumerism.

We can live simply, saying no to unnecessary material things in our outer lives. We can also work inwardly to heal the divisiveness and imbalance in the world. Our individual conscious awareness of love's oneness reconnects the split between masculine and feminine, spirit and matter, body and soul, and with the soul of the world. We can begin to heal the wounds our culture has inflicted on the Earth.

Love is the most powerful force in the universe. Love draws us back to love, love uncovers love, and love makes us whole.

In the depths of the soul, we are loved more than we know. This is the deepest secret of being human, the bond of love at the core of our being, which belongs to all that exists. And the more we live this love, the more we give ourselves to this mystery that is both human and divine, the more fully we participate in life as it really is, in its wonder and moment by moment revelation.

The Earth is a living oneness born from love, being remade by love in each instant. And we can be part of its healing, transformation, and awakening. The Earth is waiting, in need of our participation. It has been wounded by our greed and exploitation, and by our forgetfulness of its sacred nature. It needs us to remember and reconnect, to live the oneness that is our true nature.

Love is the simplest key to this oneness, this remembrance. Love is the most ordinary and most direct way to uncover what is real – the innermost secrets of life. It is at the root of all that exists, as well as in every bud breaking open at springtime, every fruit ripening in fall.

Love reminds us that we are part of life; that we belong to each other and to this living suffering planet. Love will reconnect us to the sacred ways known to our ancestors, as well as awaken us to new ways to be with each other and the Earth. We just need to say 'yes' to this mystery within our own hearts, to open to the link of love that unites us all, that is woven into the web of life. And then we will uncover the love affair that is life itself, and hear the song of unity as it comes alive in our hearts and in the heart of the world.

## Suggestions

When not used wisely, anger can cause pain to both the person who is angry and the person who is hurt, whereas love brings light. Love is divine presence, the foundation of life, existing at the root of yourself.

Love can be awakened by meditating on the heart.

The practise of remembering God realligns the unconscious by removing the blockages.

Practices:

- Fill your heart with love.
- Practise simple acts of loving kindness.
- Cook with love and care.
- Listen with an open heart.
- Touch others with tenderness.
- Go deep in prayer till you merge in love's infinite ocean.

Reawaken the power of love. Say yes to the mystery within your own heart.

# Love in a Time of Fear

SCILLA ELWORTHY

## About Scilla Elworthy

Scilla Elworthy founded the Oxford Research Group in 1982 to develop dialogue with nuclear weapons decision makers, and then set up Peace Direct in 2002 to support local peace-builders in conflict areas. Three times nominated for the Nobel Peace Prize, awarded the Niwano Peace Prize in 2003, she advised Archbishop Desmond Tutu and Sir Richard Branson in setting up 'The Elders.' She co-founded Rising Women Rising World in 2013, her latest book is *The Business Plan for Peace: building a world without war*, and her TED talk on nonviolence has been viewed by over 1,400,000 people.

# Scilla Elworthy

'How to clear anger from our system,
how to use anger for transformation,
and how to transcend anger toward love.'
—Daaji

## My story

In 1980 I was deeply afraid that a nuclear war might happen. And I was not wrong to be afraid, because in 1983 we were eighteen minutes away from *accidental* nuclear war. Soviet radar scanners observed an incoming missile attack and warned the Kremlin to launch its own missiles, when an alert colonel noticed that the supposed attack was actually a flock of geese!

So I started to act. I helped organise the Mothers' Walk for Nuclear Disarmament in Oxford, UK, and then I was sent to the United Nations in New York for the Second Special Session on Nuclear Disarmament in 1982. After two weeks of deliberations no progress had been made, and there was a massive demonstration in the streets of New York; people poured in from all over the world, as far away as Japan, and we filled Central Park from end to end.

The next morning, the New York Times gave five pages of enthusiastic coverage. I went back to my work in the UN full of enthusiasm that this would change everything.

By the end of the day, not one country had changed its position one centimeter. I was distraught that one million people asking their governments – in a totally peaceful way – to stop producing nuclear weapons and agree a treaty to build down their arsenals, had had no effect at all. I was shocked and depressed that a million citizens couldn't change this threat to the world in any way.

Then, as I was strap-hanging on a bus on Broadway, a voice in my head said 'You're talking to the wrong people. The UN can't do anything about this. You have to talk to the people who make the decisions.'

'Who are they?' I asked myself. Then it was obvious: The physicists who design the warheads, the intelligence people who insist the new weapons are necessary; the arms producers who make the missiles; the defense ministries who sign the checks; the military personnel who deploy and target the weapons; and the politicians.

So, I obeyed the voice in my head and went home and started a research group around my kitchen table, to find out 'Who makes the decisions?' in the nuclear weapons

[25] McLean, S., 1986. *How Nuclear Weapons Decisions are Made.* MacMillan, London, UK.

owners – the USA, the Soviet Union, the UK, France, and China.

To cut a long story short, once we had done four years' research and published our first book[25], we tried to engage these decision makers in dialogue. They all refused to talk to us, and again I was deeply dismayed. But now I understand why. They sensed, correctly, that we were propelled by fear, and in my case, anger. I was furious that anyone could jeopardise our future, and our children's future, by making such toxic and dangerous weapons and putting them on hair-trigger alert.

At this point in my life I learned to meditate, and deepened the self-reflection started some years before. I began to examine my shadow, my darker self, and slowly realised how angry and fearful I was. When I became conscious of that, and began to transform it over several years, people began to say yes.

By 1987, we went to Moscow with a delegation of women and had a discussion with Mikhail Gorbachev, leader of the then Soviet Union. We brought women from Eastern Europe for talks within the NATO headquarters in Brussels – the very first time anyone from Eastern Europe had been inside NATO.

The Oxford Research Group, as we were called, began to invite nuclear decision makers to an old Quaker manor house near Oxford, and they began to come. At first it was rather tense and formal, but we did our best to make it a safe place to talk, with home-cooked food and wildflowers in everybody's bedroom.

After the initial suspicion and mistrust had subsided, due to the way all participants were treated and the meetings were facilitated, participants were rolling up their sleeves and thrashing out possible terms for treaties.

It took about ten years to get to this point. One key ingredient was complete confidentiality – there were no press releases, no communiqués, and nothing of these meetings was ever reported in the media. Building trust between participants was essential. The same is true of the nuclear dialogues conducted by the Oxford Research Group today.

But there was another key ingredient – a lack of fear and anger. All of us who 'held' these meetings were not afraid of the people or the process, and we were no longer angry at them. We saw them as fellow humans struggling with a huge problem, and frequently we grew fond of them. That made all the difference.

## What are the skills needed to move from anger to love?

In half a century of work in this world of armed conflict, the most important lesson I've learned is that inner work is a prerequisite for outer effectiveness.

There are two reasons for this. One is that the quality of our awareness directly affects the quality of the results produced. The other reason is that if we haven't investigated our own shadow sides – our jealousy, anger, fear, and greed – and are not continually working to integrate them, we are likely to 'project' those unconscious emotions onto others.

Here is an example of someone Peace Direct has supported for many years. Gulalai Ismail lives in Northwest Pakistan, and since she was fifteen years old she has been helping young women to go to school, with her colleague Malala Yousefzai, who was shot in the head for doing just that. Undeterred, Gulalai now trains teams of young people to go into madrassas, locate those being trained for jihad, and go home with them to talk with their parents about why the Koran does not sanction suicide bombing. They have dissuaded over 200 potential suicide bombers from carrying out their missions. This work would not be possible without an extremely high level of self-awareness.

The new brand of leaders needed to meet the challenges of today, and thrive in the world of tomorrow, know and live the connection between inner self-development and outer action. If we want to communicate clearly, transform conflicts, generate energy, and develop trust within our families and in our places of work, our first challenge is to do the inner work.

## Self-knowledge

This is the current evolutionary challenge that many people don't yet grasp: The desired outer changes require inner change. If a critical mass of humanity can make this shift, an entirely new way of living can emerge.

The evolutionary shift is a leap in our ability to move from thinking about 'me,' to thinking about 'we.' This may seem difficult at first, but soon it becomes clear that it is a nourishing and satisfying way to live, because human beings are drawn to a sense of purpose in life. What many of us search for is a feeling of belonging, a feeling of community.

In short, we have to do deeply personal work to be less personal!

When I was 30, I contracted a brain disease that put me in a coma for two weeks and took six years of recovery. During that period, my brain was too foggy to attempt any kind of research, but there was one thought that went round and round in my head: 'Who am I?' Eventually, I found my way to a person who gave me some tools to start answering that question.

Over many decades I have found that the capacity for self-knowledge and insight is essential to prevent or resolve conflict. The greater the self-awareness, the less unresolved personal issues will taint our actions, and the greater the effectiveness of the work we do. As an obvious example, it is essential for those of us mediating between opponents not to be driven by anger or fear, but to have recognised and addressed our own darker emotions.

## Listening

More conflicts are prevented or resolved by the ability to listen than by any other means. Most of us think we are good listeners; most of us are not. When we are apparently listening, we spend most of our time thinking what we're going to say next or judging the other person or interpreting or simply not being present.

Your full undivided attention is the greatest gift you can give another person, especially in an argument. A person who feels truly heard starts to relax. Better still, if the listener is concentrating hard enough to hear the feelings behind the actual words, information emerges.

Let me offer an example. While working with the global executives of a major international company, I asked them to undertake an exercise sitting in pairs opposite one another for forty minutes. They were required to keep eye contact, and listen intently while their partners answered questions like 'What's disturbing you in your life?' 'What are you yearning for?' 'What's your highest potential?'

Each partner took a turn answering, by going well below the cognitive to the gut level, and each took a turn listening, which meant giving absolute attention.

At first they hated it. Bodies squirmed with the embarrassment of eye contact and personal honesty. By the end, they had a new take on the power of listening, and after using it at work for a few weeks the CEO reported, 'What you taught us enables us to resolve in fifteen minutes what would previously have taken four hours of argument, and still not been solved.'

So, if you have a conflict with someone and want to exercise your listening skills, you could ask them, 'Would you be willing to spend thirty minutes with me, so we can understand what's between us?' You could explain that you will listen to how they feel about the issue if they express it in the first person and without pointing the finger. Then you will feed back what you have heard, as exactly as you can. Then you will swap over: You will speak for about five minutes, and the other person will listen attentively enough to be able to repeat back to you what you have said.

What normally happens in this process is a shift from the *mind,* which says, 'I'm right and you're wrong!' to the *heart*, which says, 'Oh my goodness, is *that* how you feel?'

At that point, you may be able to talk about what you both long for, your unfulfiled needs, which are the deeper reasons for your anger, fear or jealousy. You may be able to suggest how the other person could do something to contribute to meeting your needs or to make an offer that could contribute to meeting theirs. You both can then respond.

The British government knows that what finally brought thirty years of terror to an end in Northern Ireland was not the application of superior force. It was the building of bridges, listening, patient mediation, respect, and dialogue. Senator George Mitchell, who played a major part in the eventual Good Friday Agreement, said, 'I will listen for as long as it takes.'

## The Inner Critic - how to work with it

Within all of us there are critical forces that can crush our imagination, cripple our energy, shrivel our ideas, and reduce us to helpless inaction. Apparently, even the most successful executives suffer from what is called 'imposter syndrome,' meaning they fear they will be unmasked as frauds.

These are the forces that breed anger, because when we cannot face what our critic constantly tells us is 'wrong' with us, we tend to 'project' that inadequacy onto others in the form of criticism or anger.

These are the forces we need to face and transform. It is hard work facing our inner critic, but there is a bonus! The Inner Critic often has a secret for us, below all the carping. There is a diamond under the claw of the fire-breathing dragon!

Here's a way I have found to discover that gem. Let's suppose that the Inner Critic gets traction in the following ways:

> You have a major challenge coming up, and start to doubt your abilities.
>
> You are suddenly ambushed by an incident from your past, perhaps where someone made you look foolish.
>
> A carping voice sits on your shoulder saying, 'You don't belong,' 'You're not good enough to do this,' 'You're not loved,' 'You're a fraud,' etc.

The Inner Critic can sabotage you at any time with these mutterings. So here is one way to transform it, using your courage to actually meet the dragon of your Inner Critic.

When it next wakes you in the middle of the night:

> Breathe deeply and calmly for a few minutes.
>
> Set out two cushions or chairs.

> Sit on one cushion or in one chair, and speak to your Inner Critic as if it were sitting opposite.
>
> Ask it why it is bothering you. Ask, 'What do you want of me?'
>
> Then get up and go and sit in the Inner Critic's chair. Answer as if you are the Inner Critic. It may feel a little strange, but you will find that if you give it a chance, it will speak very clearly. It will probably repeat the same kind of accusation.
>
> Go back to your own chair or cushion, and tell the Critic, 'You are not being very helpful! Please tell me what I need to know!'
>
> Then go across to the Critic's place, and answer again in the Critic's voice. It will start to give you more practical advice.
>
> Continue the process until you have heard and digested what it says.
>
> Then, see if you can agree on a plan with the Critic, one that is comfortable and possible for you to carry out.

When I keep going with this process, I have always found that the Critic has exceptional wisdom – it knows something that I need to know in that situation.

## Presence

When it comes to political issues, we often get caught in a cycle of self-righteousness or blame that keeps us stuck – an attitude that can obliterate any prospect of real dialogue with those holding different points of view.

While working on nuclear weapons I became acquainted with my own self-righteousness intimately – the captivating, invigorating notion that I am right and 'they' are wrong.

The moral high ground is not a good place to be. It is neither useful nor effective. I have realised painfully over the years that if I genuinely want to open a dialogue with someone, I have to be open to accept what they are saying to me, *and to even consider the awful possibility that I might be wrong!*

'Presence' might not sound like a big word, but it saves lives. Here is a true story:

In 2003, shortly after the invasion of Iraq, U.S. Lieutenant Colonel Chris Hughes was leading his men down a street in Najaf, when suddenly people came pouring out of the houses and mosques lining the street. They were furiously angry, screaming, and waving their fists. The heavily armed soldiers, most of them about nineteen years old and speaking no Arabic, had no idea what was happening. Chris Hughes instantly saw a massacre in the making. He strode into the middle of the crowd, raised his rifle above his head, pointing the barrel at the ground, and shouted an order to his men that they had never heard before: 'Kneel!' The bewildered troops, burdened by their heavy body armor, wobbled to the ground and pointed their rifles into the sand.

[26] The full story is told by Dan Baum: 'Battle Lessons: What the Generals Don't Know,' *The New Yorker*, January 17, 2005. www.newyorker.com/archive/2005/01/17/050117

The crowd quieted in disbelief, and there was absolute stillness for some two minutes. Then the crowd dispersed.[26]

This gesture of respect averted a bloodbath. No weapons were needed, no shots were fired, no revenge was required. What did we learn?

> Many furious conflicts are caused by humiliation.
>
> Respect is usually the most effective antidote to humiliation.
>
> To show respect to someone who has angered and humiliated us is challenging; it requires compassion, self-awareness, and presence.

When we're suddenly faced with a crisis, like a knife fight in the street, presence is required, which means being calm in the face of turbulence, upheaval, fear, and anger.

Learning the skills to do that requires practise. Deep breathing needs to become an automatic reaction, as it calms the mind and allows the heart to do its work. Moving to the heart instead of the head is a better bet; while the head tends to panic, the heart knows how to understand what's happening in the psyche of the other people involved. Once we can be present to what's happening in the people causing the violence, we have a much greater chance of meeting them rather than fighting them.

Such a response is demanding. Families of knife crime victims might find it difficult to accept such an approach. For all of us, the hope would be not to have to use these skills, but we need to practise them so that they're available when such things arise.

If you're suddenly severely criticised by a professor, a superior or even a colleague, you need to be able to call on your inner resources, your presence, rather than reacting. When in a very tight corner, you want to be able to switch to empathy, and really feel what the other is feeling. This is unusual, and it is a radical act.

On a larger scale, we know that true presence, resulting from regular self-reflection, is essential to the effectiveness of what we do in the world. At Peace Direct, we have recorded countless examples of how peace-building initiatives succeed best when local heroes use such skills.[27]

It took harsh experiences as a child soldier in DR Congo for Henri Bura Ladyi to acquire these skills. He was kidnapped by the militia, and then escaped, fleeing through the bush where he was eventually sheltered by the Centre for Conflict Resolution. With care and education, he learned to feel safe again, and then decided to dedicate the rest of his life to freeing other abducted young people.

When Peace Direct is able to send Henri a small amount of money, he rides his bike into the bush, buys a herd of goats, and drives them to where the militia are encamped. This means risking his life, because the militia are trigger-happy, high on drugs, and don't like intruders. But Henri knows how to contain fear, and his presence in itself enables him to negotiate; he barters one goat for one child and brings each child back to their family.

[27] www.peacedirect.org

Then the hard work begins, because re-integration of these traumatised teenagers, who have often been forced to murder people from their own village, is complex and takes time. One of the best methods Henri has found is for the kids to be given work on a village project nearby, where their relatives can see that they want to serve and become whole again.

## Anger as the fuel for transformation

Anger is like gasoline. If you spray it over people and light a match, there will be an inferno. People will get hurt. But if you put it in your engine, like fuel contained in a carburetor, it will drive you forward. It can enable you to pick yourself up when everything goes wrong. It can get you up in the morning when you feel too tired to go on facing the music.

But we need to be constantly aware of our anger, and constantly cleaning it. By that I mean watching carefully to see that the anger is not personalised, that it is not directed at an individual but at an action, at some wrong that is being done.

Then it will be clean, and it can cut through the rationalisations and explanations, and demand change.

That is anger working on behalf of love.

## Scilla Elworthy

### Anger, fear, and love today

Many of us feel afraid today. We seem to be living in a world in crisis. We are faced by the challenges of our time, those man-made financial, societal, and environmental crises that seem to be getting worse.

Many of us feel angry that waste is polluting our oceans, that not enough is being done about global warming, and that human beings are ruining the planet to such an extent that we may become extinct.

Many of us feel helpless today, even hopeless in face of the huge challenges facing us.

But the people we love and admire are those who have the courage to act, to do something, however small or grand, to change what seems overwhelming. We love those who speak out about the issues, and face the criticism they receive. We love those who find good practical solutions and carry them out. In this time of confusion, we love and admire their courage and their wisdom.

And why do we love them? Because that's what we all are below the surface. We are all made of love, every single body is a miracle, everything we might not like is ultimately capable of transformation, every time we look at a flower or a tree, all we see is love at work.

## *Suggestions*

Inner work is a prerequisite for outer effectiveness. The quality of your awareness directly affects the quality of the results.

To manage anger, first investigate your shadow side. The capacity for self-knowledge and insight is essential to prevent and resolve conflict.

If you have an argument with someone, listen. Your full undivided attention is the greatest gift you can give them. A person who feels truly heard starts to relax. Retain respect for those who have angered or humiliated you. To do this, move to the heart instead of the head, as the heart knows how to understand the underlying causes.

Anger can drive you forward. It can enable you to pick yourself up when everything goes wrong. Continually clean your anger. Let anger work on behalf of love.

# Love Is All

SATISH KUMAR

## About Satish Kumar

A former monk and long-term peace and environment activist, Satish Kumar has been quietly setting the global agenda for change for over 50 years. He was 9 when he left his family home to join the wandering Jains, and 18 when he decided he could achieve more back in the world, campaigning for land reform in India and working to turn Gandhi's vision of a renewed India and a peaceful world into reality.

In his early 20s, Satish embarked on an 8,000-mile peace pilgrimage. Carrying no money and depending on the kindness and hospitality of strangers, he walked from India to America, via Moscow, London and Paris, to deliver a humble packet of 'peace tea' to the then leaders of the world's four nuclear powers.

In 1973, Satish settled in the United Kingdom, taking up the post of editor of *Resurgence* magazine, a position he has held ever since. During this time, he has been the guiding spirit behind a number of now internationally respected ecological and educational ventures, including Schumacher College in South Devon, where he is still a Visiting Fellow. In his 50th year, Satish undertook another pilgrimage, again carrying no money. This time, he walked 2,000 miles to the holy places of Britain, a venture he describes as a celebration of his love of life and nature.

His autobiography, *No Destination*, was published in 1978. He is also the author of *You Are, Therefore I Am: A Declaration of Dependence*, *The Buddha and the Terrorist*, and *Earth Pilgrim*.

Satish has appeared regularly in the printed media, on radio, in documentaries, and on TV. He is on the advisory board of Our Future Planet, and is vice president of the RSPCA. He continues to teach and run workshops on reverential ecology, holistic education, and voluntary simplicity, and is a much sought-after speaker.

'If I have a faith that can move mountains,
but have not love, I am nothing.'
—Corinthians, The Bible

## What is love?

Life is a landscape of love, and love is the celebration of life. Love is the means, and love is the end. Love is our way and it is our destination. There is no way to love: Love is the way and love is the goal. Love is a way of being. Love is a way of life.

When we are in love, we are in love all the time. We are in love every moment. The moment we wake up, we fall in love with each other and with life itself. Falling in love is not a one-day event, it is an everyday event. Love never ends. Love endures. We are spellbound by the mystery of love forever. It's love for the sake of loving. There is no other motivation. Love is not logic; love is pure magic. Love is pure poetry and pure pleasure.

Love is sacred. Love is unlimited and unconditional. Allow yourself to be swept away by the force of love. True love is to love even when your beloved is less than perfect. It is easy to love someone who is good and perfect. But true love is to love even those who may not be so good. To love is to be free from criticising, complaining, and comparing. To practise universal love is to recognise that those who behave badly do so because they have not been loved. W.H. Auden goes even further when he says, 'Those to whom evil is done do evil in return.' Those who are loved, love in return. Let us create a monsoon of love and nourish all living beings. Only through the act of loving do we teach others how to love.

When Christ said, 'Love your enemy,' he did not say it lightly. He was serious. He believed that '*Amor vincit omnia*,' meaning 'Love conquers all.' By love, enemy becomes friend. Love keeps no record of wrong doings. Love is not a path for the faint-hearted. Love requires courage – courage to turn the other cheek. To love is to be brave. Sing the song of love and all your worries and miseries will evaporate! Live in the ecstasy of love. Then you will be sustained by love.

## Love as acceptance

Love is the acceptance of oneself as one is, and acceptance of the other as the other is. Acceptance without expectation, without judgment and without qualification. Love, free of expectations, encounters no disappointment. Love is to accept bitter with sweet, dark with light, pain with pleasure, all with equanimity. The moment we bring love into our hearts, we transform illusion into imagination, and duality into unity. We transcend from likes and dislikes, and we enter into the celebration of life as it is. When we drink the sweet nectar of love, there is a transformation. As Jalal Ad-Din Rumi, the Sufi poet, said,

> By love, the bitter becomes sweet;
> By love, copper becomes gold;

By love, the dregs become clear;
By love, pain becomes healing.
This is the transformative power of love.

To love is to see God, because God is love and love is God. To mystics and Sufi poets, God appears as the beloved and the beloved as God. Love is the greatest religion on Earth. Love is the mother of all virtues; peace and compassion, generosity and humility are born from love. Love is majestic and magnificent. Where there is love, there is hope. Love and rejoice.

## Start with yourself

Where do we start our journey of love? We start with ourselves. Christ said, 'Love your neighbor as yourself.' The word 'yourself' is the key. As you love yourself, love others. The 'other' is only an extension of yourself. Loving your 'self' is not selfish! If you cannot love yourself, how can you love someone else, and why should you expect someone else to love you?

Accepting yourself as you are, and loving yourself for being who you are, are prerequisites for loving others as they are and who they are. We are made of each other.

Lovers take no offence and give no offence. Lovers take no enemies, make no enemies, and have no enemies. Animosity is a consequence of hate and friendship is the consequence of love. As bees love flowers and produce honey, lovers love each other and produce happiness. Love is the purpose of life and through love we find the meaning of life.

To live is to love, and to love is to risk – to risk being hurt, to risk the possibility of not being loved in return. Do not wish to have a lover, simply be a lover. Having a lover is a result of being a lover.

Love awakens the soul, love nourishes the heart, love brings joy to our lives. Love is the most beautiful mantra of the mind. The balm of love heals all wounds, the wounds of anger and anxiety, the wounds of fear and resentment.

Love of yourself, love of your beloved, love of people and love of Nature is a continuum. We need to be kind to ourselves and to all others so that no one needs to be subjected to suffering and everyone can experience the joy of love.

Love is as natural to us as breathing. Rumi says, 'Your task is not to seek for love but merely to seek and find all the barriers within yourself that you have built against love.'

This all-embracing love manifests through many forms, such as philology (love of learning), philosophy (love of wisdom), and philanthropy (love of people).

More intimately, we experience erotic love. How beautiful it is to fall in love and be in the embrace of one's beloved! 'I love you' is the most powerful and most beautiful sentence in the entire English language. Falling in love is not an event that takes place only once in a lifetime. If we want, we can and we should fall in love every day, even with the same beloved. By loving one, we love all. Falling in love is a miracle. We are born thanks to the act of making love.

Everyone is a love child. There is no original sin, only original love.

Poets, artists, and mystics experience the ecstasy of romantic love physically, emotionally, imaginatively, and spiritually. Romantic poetry and art celebrate our heart connections with each other, with nature and with humans. Love takes us beyond reason, beyond intellect, and beyond description. Love brings us to a place beyond right and wrong, a place of magnanimity and generosity. This is deep love of life. All we need is love because love is all and everything. Love is the answer. What is your question?

## Suggestions

Love is an everyday event. True love is to love even when your beloved is less than perfect. Refrain from criticising, complaining, and comparing. Love is acceptance without expectation, judgment or qualification.

Through the act of loving, you will teach others how to love.

Love is the mother of all virtues. To love is to see God.

Start with yourself. Accept yourself as you are.

# The Positive Side of Anger

RUBY CARMEN

## About Ruby Carmen

Ruby is a certified meditation trainer with the Heartfulness Institute. Her educational background includes a B.A. (Hons) in Psychology and Sociology from the University of Strathclyde, and M.Ed. in Psychology and Education from the University of Cambridge. A member of the British Psychological Society, the main focus of her professional life has been in working with minority ethnic groups and refugees, with a particular emphasis on mental health. Her current work focuses on training in the use of meditation as a vehicle for self-development and as means of enhancing individual and collective well-being. Her languages include Hindi, Urdu, Punjabi, French, German, and English.

## A psychological perspective

All of us are familiar with anger. It is one of the basic human emotions, and while most of us are able to see it in others, it is more complex when it comes to recognising it in ourselves. Cultural and social conditioning also play a role in shaping and defining the 'line' of acceptable displays of anger.

Personally, I have found anger to be a troublesome friend or, I should say, enemy. I have learned to ask the feeling when it arises, 'Why have you come, and what do I need to learn from you?' But before sharing my own story, I want to examine some psychological aspects of anger, as psychology has been an intrinsic part of my life, as has spirituality.

In the 1970s, researchers and psychologists like Ekman[28] identified six basic emotions. One of them was anger, and the others were happiness, sadness, fear, disgust, and surprise. You may not be surprised at this list. Other theorists and psychologists, such as Plutchik, proposed a rainbow wheel of emotions where there are combined emotions in varying degrees of intensity. From experience,

[28] Ekman, P., 1999. Basic emotions. T. Dalgleish & M. J. Power (Eds.), *Handbook of Cognition and Emotion*, Editors: T. Dalgleish & M. J. Power, pp. 45–60. John Wiley & Sons Ltd.

we often identify with this rainbow of emotional complexity, as usually our emotions and feelings are mixed up in any given situation. For example, we can love someone and equally be irritated with their behavior.

There are a multitude of theories to explain human emotions, and the intention here is not to share all of them. There are evolutionary theories, physiological theories, and cognitive theories. One theorist was Richard Lazarus[29], who developed the cognitive appraisal theory of emotion. He proposed that a sequence happens with an emotion: first, there is a stimulus, then a thought, which leads to a simultaneous physiological response and emotion.

In more recent years, and also touching on yogic psychology[30], there is a discourse around feelings (and emotions) being 'information,' as well as energy. Our feelings, as real as they seem, as visceral as they seem, are information but not necessarily facts. They are usually a response to a trigger, which can exist externally or internally. Our thoughts can also sometimes act as an internal trigger. So, an event itself can be 'neutral,' but our thinking makes it 'good' or 'bad,' echoing the advice of the ancients including the Stoic philosophers.

Coming back to anger more specifically, it is a powerful emotion that is related to our 'flight-or-fight' and 'freeze'

[29] Lazarus, R. S., 2000. Cognitive-motivational-relational theory of emotion. *Emotions in Sport*, Editor Y.L. Hannin, pp. 39–63. Human Kinetics.

[30] Patel, K.D., 2019. Yogic Psychology. *Heartfulness*, Vol. 4, 12. Sahaj Marg Spirituality Foundation, India.

responses. It is also characterised by agitation, frustration, antagonism, and a response to a perceived threat (real or imagined). Moreover, when a threat is perceived, anger serves as a means of dealing with danger and protecting ourselves and others. In this light, anger's function is to necessitate some kind of action.

Anger becomes problematic when it is our default response, rather than an adaptive call to action. When it is problematic, we speak of 'anger management issues,' with suppressed anger turning into the more toxic form of rage.

## My story

In recent years, after many years of meditation practice and working on myself[31], it came to light that I had suppressed long-held feelings of anger that had transformed into rage, even pure fury. It surprised me, like an uninvited, unloved, and unwanted guest. Following multiple surgeries for a chronic illness, I had prematurely entered menopause, and with this upheaval and the physiological and hormonal changes in my body, anger and rage began to seep out, sometimes when I least expected them. I was so troubled by this that my sleep was disturbed, and I felt quite unable to deal with such a force of anger.

All cognitive psychological theories and possible explanations appeared unhelpful and useless. Why? Surely, all the psychological tools, knowledge and understanding,

[31] Patel, K.D. and J. Pollock, 2018. *The Heartfulness Way: Heart-based Meditations for Spiritual Transformation*. New Harbinger, USA.

spiritual techniques, and coping strategies that I had adopted over time would help me. Well, not quite, actually, and I will come back to this.

Across most cultures, anger has been seen as an inherently negative emotion, at least until recent times. Now we recognise that anger can be constructive, even transformative in nature. It depends on what we *do* with the feelings of anger. When we harm ourselves or others, then we deem it to be 'negative,' whereas when anger is used to constructively bring about change in ourselves then the anger is akin to a catalyst for transformation. With this approach, anger acts as a form of information. Something is not right and needs our attention. It needs to change in order for us to grow.

Anger is then adaptive and transformative. Within the scope of our control or influence, all that we can change is ourselves. This lesson has appeared time and time again, through years of meditation practice and working in the field of mental health and emotional well-being. The only thing we can change is ourselves and our reactions.

I have consciously and unconsciously avoided anger for the greatest part of my life; I would avoid being angry and also avoid angry people. In part, that can be understood in the context of growing up with an emotionally damaged and abusive parent. From a young age, my raison d'être was to be the peacemaker, coupled with an intense inner longing for balance, harmony, and peace. In addition, the multicultural environment I inhabited for over a decade also determined my relationship with anger. Anger is not befitting for a young woman; it is not 'ladylike' in the bi-cultural existence I inhabited.

As a result of these gender and cultural restraints, my anger was left unexpressed, unsaid, and ignored, until it could be contained no more. Jokingly, I would remark to close friends that 'I am not an angry person, but when I *do* get angry, it is like Vesuvius erupting!' Explosive, short-lived, and cathartic would best describe it.

## The role of thought

Some psychologists and theorists claim that anger is a second-hand emotion. They believe that other emotions like fear, grief, and our response to pain precede the anger response, and that anger occurs when some form of pain presents itself along with triggering thoughts. In this framework, we can examine the role of thought.

Do our thoughts create our anger? From ancient times, the Stoic philosophers and the yogis of India have stated that the external trigger is essentially neutral; rather, it is our thinking and subsequent reaction that leads to anger. In this vein, if we change our thinking about a situation we perceive as negative, harmful or threatening, will our anger decrease? Are we able to replace anger with self-compassion and compassion for the trigger? Of course, at a very human level it is an emotional labor, yet if we do a cost-benefit analysis of the effects of anger on our well-being, it can be argued that it is worth the effort.

I am reminded of a quote, often attributed to Lord Buddha, but in fact from the twelve-step program of AA: 'Holding onto anger is like drinking poison and expecting the other to die.'

The 'holding on' part is key here. As mentioned earlier, anger can be helpful and can create the impetus or catalyst for change – for example, to leave the job with which you have become disenchanted after your boss or colleague insults you one time too many!

After many years, I realised that I had been repressing a lot of anger, pain, and grief, and it was causing me harm and adding to my chronic pain condition. This realisation did not happen overnight; rather, it unfolded and continues to unfold. At one point, I came to a juncture in my life where I could no longer hold it within me. I could no longer live that way; the need for self-expression, complete honesty, and authenticity became so essential, so vital to my being. For authenticity to be expressed, the anger needed to be released and, more significantly, accepted: 'Yes, this too is a part of me.' Then I could start to heal.

## We are hardwired for fairness

The ancient philosophers viewed anger as a proto passion related to desire, which often came with the intention for revenge, particularly when the person felt wronged or an injustice had been committed. I am sure that we can all recall times when we have felt righteous anger: 'He should not have spoken or behaved like that. How dare he!' Modern psychology concurs with this – we believe a 'rule' has been broken. Here the dualities of right versus wrong, and good versus bad, come into play through our judgments on others and ourselves. There is another lesson in this for me, as I am often painfully aware of the stream of self-judgment that shows up in my consciousness, sometimes out of the blue.

Following this line of analysis, anger manifests from injustice. Alongside it is the perception of threat or potential harm, and here is where anger and fear may blend into one another. Recently, neuroscientists have suggested that we humans are hardwired for fairness, and we actively resist what we perceive as injustice. This is a fascinating viewpoint and speaks of a mainly positive model of humanity – that we are inherently social beings.

## My favourite anger strategies

Whether we believe anger is a basic human emotion or a second-hand emotion, what matters is how we deal with it on a day-to-day basis. A practical approach is needed, so here are some strategies that have been helpful to me personally:

Radical compassion – compassion toward individuals and, in particular, toward my own self. This self-compassion is something that is an ongoing effort until ultimately it becomes effortless and natural.

If I feel myself becoming angry, justified or not, I pause and take time to ask, 'What is needed in this moment?' Really truly listening to what that is or even simply pausing, can be beneficial. It is part and parcel of some of the Cognitive Behavioral Therapy techniques of self-monitoring, self-awareness, cognitive distancing, and 'postponement,' that is, suggesting to myself to wait for the anger to release (like air from a balloon) before I act.

Breathing exercises support this and help me to regulate the body into a more balanced state rather than the fight-or-flight response.

The concept of postponing action until anger has dissipated is believed to have come from the Pythagoreans and was then adopted by the Stoics centuries later. Now it is used in modern psychotherapy[32].

Anger management approaches always advocate creating space between us and the trigger. Walking in nature, grounding ourselves in the natural world, can be so helpful in soothing the thoughts, feelings, and sensations created by anger. During the months of lockdown, walking near where I live, taking time to appreciate the natural beauty, the trees, flowers, swans, mountains, sky, and the caress of sunshine on my face has been priceless.

During the pandemic, I began training in Heartful Communication and Nonviolent Communication (NVC), and this opened up new vistas of understanding about the radical compassion and acceptance mentioned earlier. The founder of NVC, Marshall Rosenberg, speaks of anger thus[33]: 'If we wish to express anger fully, the first step is to divorce the other person from any responsibility for our anger.' That is, take full responsibility for your own feelings, needs and longings, and avoid the blame game. 'Get curious, not furious,' is the phrase used in NVC. It is an invitation to make a shift in consciousness and practise

[32] Robertson, D., 2020. *How to Think Like a Roman Emperor: The Stoic Philosophy of Marcus Aurelius*. St. Martin's Press.

compassion, empathy, and ultimately see yourself in the other – no 'them and us,' only 'us.'

While I aspire to radical acceptance, radical compassion, and empathy, I am still a work in progress. There is an inner shift, and perhaps it could be called an attitudinal change. I have become more accepting of anger and am no longer afraid of it. Anger is part of life, and it can be triggered in me at any moment, even every day. When I treat it as a messenger or 'visitor,' I can deal with it, learn from it, and grow from it rather than allowing it to be destructive. It helps me understand where I need to grow and expand, offering myself and others more empathy and love. In summary, anger need not be our enemy. We can make friends with it and use it as wisely as possible to examine what has gone wrong, and where change is needed in order to become a more loving human being.

[33] Rosenberg, M.B., 2003. *Nonviolent Communication: A Language of Life*. PuddleDancer Press, USA.

## *Suggestions*

Anger necessitates action. It is problematic only when the default reaction is destructive rather than an adaptive call to action. Suppressed anger can become toxic rage, whereas adaptive anger can be a catalyst for transformation. You can only change yourself and your reactions.

Neuroscientists suggest that we are hardwired for fairness and we resist injustice.

Treat anger as a messenger, a visitor. Divorce the other person from responsibility for your anger. Shift your awareness.

Practices:

- When you feel anger rising, ask yourself, 'Why have you come, and what do I need to learn from you?'
- Do breathing exercises to deactivate the sympathetic nervous system's fight or flight response and recreate balance.
- Create space between yourself and the trigger.
- Walk in nature to ground yourself.
- Practise radical compassion, including self-compassion. Ask, 'What is needed in this moment?'
- Wait for the feelings of anger to be released before acting.

# From Disruption to Love in the Midst of Chaos

VASCO GASPAR

## About Vasco Gaspar

With a degree in Psychology from the University of Coimbra, Vasco is the author of the book, *Aqui e Agora – Mindfulness*. He works internationally as a facilitator and speaker in the areas of conscious leadership and human potential, in the private, public, and voluntary sectors. He has directly reached more than 30,000 people around the world. His main interest lies in the integration of different contemplative practices, such as Mindfulness, Heartfulness and Presencing, with proven practices of psychotherapy, neuroscience and others, at the service of the highest human potential applied for the greater good.

He is certified by several renowned institutes such as the Presencing Institute, Heartfulness Institute, Search Inside Yourself Leadership Institute and IFS Institute, among others. He holds the intention of inspiring change and transformation towards a more human and compassionate world for all living beings.

## A perfect storm

I first wrote these words in the midst of the Covid-19 pandemic in 2020. Looking back, it is interesting to observe how quickly the world has changed. How fast the things we took for granted suddenly disappeared. Even the very normal most 'unnoticed' things, like going for a walk or giving a hug to a loved one. The world was in suspension mode on one hand, and was changing drastically fast on the other.

Our lives have always been impermanent. As the Greek philosopher Heraclitus said, 'Change is the only constant in life.' But this was different. The change was global, affecting everyone directly or indirectly at the same time, as health care systems were pushed to their limits, schools were closed, and the global economic system showed how fragile it is. Millions of people died, and entire industries are still suffering a severe impact, leaving hundreds of millions without jobs. Our lifestyles must change. Many people have suffered, feeling a mix of emotions such as fear, despair, frustration, and anger.

On top of all these difficulties and emotions, we were asked to isolate and practise physical distancing. Being confined at home was almost like being asked to watch the 'normal world' collapse while seated on the couch, feeling impotent to act.

This intensified the already challenging emotions. We are social beings and relationships with others are one of the most important ingredients for our mental well-being, as several studies show. Loneliness and lack of social contact increase inflammation, depression, and dementia, and the impact manifests not only during a crisis. They also lead to Post-Traumatic Stress Disorder, as psychiatrist Bessel van der Kolk's work suggests[34], when we go through catastrophes like the one we were living, confined in limited space.

I heard from a famous TV reporter in Portugal that his father died in hospital from a disease not related to Covid-19, but he wasn't allowed to be present, to hold his hand during his last breath. Even the funeral was restricted to a small number of people and hugs were not allowed. A screaming silent distance. For most of us, touch is something very important. It helps to regulate our emotions and allows us to feel connected. All newborns need touch as much as they need water and food to survive. So, we were going against our very nature as mammals and humans.

While isolation stressed us, the other extreme was also very challenging: several generations living under the same roof in very poor conditions, sometimes sharing space with someone you didn't love any more or being a victim of domestic violence. Parents were educating their kids from home while working remotely, and it was easy to feel that personal space was invaded. Without being able to go outside for a walk to cool down, that led to arguments and violence. For some,

[34] https://onbeing.org/programs/bessel-van-der-kolk-how-trauma-lodges-in-the-body/

home was not a safe place. And there were those who didn't even have a home or the resources to buy what they needed to survive during this unusual time.

It was a perfect storm for mental illness, especially as most of us have not been taught how to regulate our minds and emotions, either in our day-to-day lives or during a crisis, when we enter into survival mode.

We were told to wash our hands and practise social distancing so as not to be infected and to not infect others, but no one told us to wash our minds and our emotions. To be grounded, centreed, present, able to connect, and compassionate, washing our emotions is as important as washing our hands, since emotions are also contagious, especially fear, anxiety, and anger.

## Co-regulation

As social beings, our nervous system has evolved in the last 500 million years to respond to threats in the environment, optimising for survival. One of the main cues we pick up from the outside world is the emotional state of others around us. We co-regulate each other, for better and for worse.

Imagine for a moment that you are a medical doctor who just came home from working in a hospital or a grocery clerk who spent the whole day making sure that people can buy their essential goods. Even today, after the pandemic, you would probably wash your hands or take a shower and put your clothes in the laundry before you interact with your family. You don't want them to be exposed to something you've brought from the outside world. But do you wash the fear, the anxiety, the frustration, and all the other emotional impressions you've accumulated during the day? If you don't, those impressions remain attached to you and will potentially infect the ones around you.

You don't need to be on the frontline to pick up those emotions. If you are not careful, they will visit you from the media, with the aggravation of fake news, which these days is even more dangerous than any biological threat. Even if you don't want to be impacted by negative impressions, at the subconscious level your autonomic nervous system (ANS) is always scanning the environment through a process called neuroception. When it identifies a potential threat from outside, like an angry person or negative news or from a negative thought inside, it activates a survival response and prepares your resources to respond accordingly.

What are these responses? According to the level of safety the system perceives, it can activate one of three responses

1. The most ancient one, which emerged around 500 million years ago, is the **immobilisation or dissociation response, also known as the freeze response.** It is activated when we sense that there is nothing we can do. It tries to shut down the system so that we dissociate from danger. The branch of the ANS responsible for it is the dorsal vagal response, associated with the parasympathetic nervous system.

   In some cases, it can even make us faint, the same way some animals faint and pretend to be dead so that they won't be attacked by predators. It is like going to our 'caves' and waiting for the storm to pass. At the psychological level, it activates states that feel depressed, without energy, helpless or that dissociate us from reality. That is why many people spend time continuously distracted on the Internet by all kinds of things. Streaming services thrived during the pandemic!

2. Around 400 million years ago, a new option emerged, known as **the fight or flight response or the mobilisation response.** Here, the sympathetic nervous system is activated to deal with the threat, either by fighting or by fleeing according to an evaluation of the risk. When this response is activated, some people feel anger and frustration (fight) or fear and anxiety (flee), and some develop panic attacks. Hormones like adrenaline and cortisol flush our system, blood pressure and muscle tension increase, and blood moves to our limbs, so that we can fight or run away.

   Mentally we become more alert, and even neutral stimuli can be interpreted as potential threats. Studies show that if we show a neutral face to someone who is in this sympathetic mode, they usually perceive it as threatening. Even the bones of the middle ear change their position in order to be more alert to high and low frequencies typically associated with predators, reducing the capacity to hear middle frequencies, like the sound of the human voice. That is why people under stress tend to have a reduced capacity to hear each other.

3. Around 200 million years ago, a new response emerged – one of connection, feeling safe, being

socially engaged with each other, which enabled cooperation. This is known as **the ventral vagal response,** and it is also part of the parasympathetic nervous system. This is the response that allows health, growth, social engagement, restoration, as well as individual and collective regulation. This is when we reach out to help each other.

It is important to understand how our ANS works so that we can actively regulate ourselves in the midst of a crisis, as well as help others to regulate themselves, given that we are social beings, and our systems influence each other.

So, coming back to the pandemic, most of us were confined at home, and the only sources of information we received were from the media and social media. Both sources are skewed to show worst-case scenarios. In the face of that information, the human neuroception mechanism running under our 'conscious radar' sensed threats and activated an appropriate response – fight or flight.

On top of that, as one of my teachers used to say, we are descendants of the 'nervous monkeys.' He used to add jokingly that the 'chilled monkeys' didn't make it! Our minds are by default thinking about what can go wrong. We are masters of anticipating worst-case scenarios because that has been important for survival. This inner condition also impacts our ANS, which again activates resources accordingly to deal with the situation, for example, the release of adrenaline so that we can flee.

We were faced with an explosive combination. The outside world feeding us everything that is going wrong (number of deaths, lockdowns, stock market meltdown, social polarisation, etc.), and the inner world anticipating worst-case scenarios and sometimes even elaborating on conspiracy theories, possible wars, and other similar hypotheses.

## Self-regulation

This hyper-activation of the threat mode led us toward the first two survival responses: By activating the fight or flight response, our system would be flooded with emotions like anxiety or anger; by activating the freeze response, we would numb ourselves, feel hopeless, depressed, and disconnected. Sometimes we activated both at the same time, which led to a state of freezing like a deer facing the headlights of a car.

Both these responses took us out of the ventral vagal response associated with feeling safe and connected. They also disconnected our capacity to access our prefrontal cortex, which is the part of our brain that allows us to think clearly, manage our impulses, feel empathy toward others, regulate and balance ourselves, and have a sense of morality – basically, what allows us to be centred, connected, wise, and compassionate. This is what we associate with our deeply human values.

Some might argue that, in the middle of a real crisis like humanity faced, a survival response was adequate. That is true in some sense. However, those first two responses evolved to deal with clear, identified threats, like lions chasing us or objects hurtling in our direction. They did not help us deal with an invisible virus. In fact, the fight or flight response negatively impacts the functioning of the immune system, which is the last thing we needed when fighting a virus.

Being angry didn't solve any problems. It even led people to act in ways that were inappropriate, such as the discrimination against Asian people in some countries. Being anxious also did not solve anything. A little dose of anxiety and fear might have helped us to be more conscious of our actions (for example, wearing masks so as not to infect others), but in larger doses they impacted our ability to think clearly, to relate with others, and even to relate with ourselves.

Finally, being disconnected and constantly distracted, 'waiting for the storm to pass,' only postponed what needed to be done in the moment.

## What can we do differently going forward?

More than ever, we need to be able to regulate ourselves – regulate our minds, regulate our bodies, regulate our systems. This means being able to activate and connect with our healthy core, our ventral response, our Heart, the place in us that has wisdom, clarity, and compassion. And from that space, to have an action in the world that is beneficial for all and that can truly help improve the current situation.

Only by regulating ourselves can we think clearly and use our resources wisely. Only from that space can we relate at a human level. In a moment of crisis, how do we show up?

As a solid harbour of sanity, kindness, and wisdom or as a source of contagion of toxic emotions and behaviors?

Some of you might be thinking, 'Easier said than done! How can I regulate myself and wash my emotions as easily as I wash my hands?' It is a fair question, given that most of us have not been taught how to use simple practices in that regard.

Fortunately, there are now many possibilities. First of all, we need to be aware which state we are at in any moment – to be mindful of our inner condition, our thoughts, emotions, and physical response. Then, if our condition is not one that suits the need of the moment, we can adjust ourselves. Sometimes, with simple breathing practices, we can 'up-regulate' our physiology, putting more energy into the system, and this is useful if we notice that we are in the freeze dorsal vagal response; or we can 'down-regulate' ourselves when there is a hyper-activation of emotions like anger or anxiety.

If we notice that we are filled with emotional impressions, leading our minds to be flooded with difficult thoughts or emotions, there is a practice called Cleaning in the Heartfulness tradition that is specifically designed to clean all the heavy emotional impressions we have gathered during the day. We can also ask for a meditation session with a trainer, to regulate our minds and take this Cleaning even deeper.

And we can also be proactive, cultivating an inner balance so as not to be so easily deregulated. Other Heartfulness practices like Meditation and Prayer help us to connect with our centre, with something higher. This activates the ventral vagal response, so that we feel more centred, more aligned, more at peace, and more compassionate.

And we don't need to shave our heads and go to a monastery for that. These are simple practices that are designed for everyday life, to help us act in ways that are more aligned and more beneficial for the whole. Their purpose is to connect us with what really matters; to guide our actions from that place of sanity and clarity. That is what the world needs now, more than ever – people who can think clearly, who can be centres of wisdom and compassion, who can help themselves and the ones around them to collectively make decisions and actions in a direction of regeneration and healthy growth.

## Beauty in the midst of chaos

Yes, there is still a crisis. Yes, there is uncertainty. Yes, there are difficult emotions – fear, pain, and anxiety. But there are also possibilities. There are new beginnings. There are people reaching out to each other and making this world a better place.

If we tune in, we can see beautiful examples; everyday heroes who are acting in the world from that space of the Heart, that space of sanity[35]. Even in the midst of chaos we have a choice. We can choose to go for the automatic

[35] See some examples at https://www.karunavirus.org/

survival responses of fight, flight, freeze or faint or we can pause, access our healthy core, connect to our hearts, and act in the world in a way that can be of benefit to the greater good.

The choice is yours. Who do you want to be? A focus of disruption and chaos or a fountain of wisdom and Love? The answer is in your hands, your heads and, especially, in your Heart.

## *Suggestions*

We have all been changed by the pandemic, and mental well-being has been negatively affected. We are living in a pandemic of mental illness. Learn to wash your emotions like you wash your hands.

Become aware of how your emotions are co-regulating with those of other people around you. Become aware of how your autonomic nervous system is scanning the environment through neuroception.

Practices:

- Become aware of your current state. Be mindful.
- Then adjust yourself by:

  Breathing exercises
  Heartfulness Cleaning
  Meditation
  Centring yourself

Look for the possibilities in every situation. You have a choice to either let your autonomic nervous system react or to pause and respond with centredness.

# Anger as Trauma's Messenger

MARILYN CORNELIUS

## About Marilyn Cornelius

Marilyn is a life coach, facilitator, speaker, author, and teacher. She is founder of Alchemus Prime, a multinational leadership and wellness company. She integrates behavioral sciences, design thinking, biomimicry, and meditation techniques to support women's empowerment, change management, trauma healing, leadership development, and climate change mitigation and adaptation.

Marilyn is the author of 32 popular books spanning topics such as self-love, positivity, trauma, leadership, healthy eating, and meditation. Her speaking engagements include Heartfulness seminars, UN women's forums, TV and radio shows.

Marilyn holds a doctorate in behavioral sciences and climate change from Stanford University's Emmett Interdisciplinary Program in Environment and Resources (E-IPER). She also holds a B.Sc. in business and environmental resource management and an Associate of Arts degree in graphic design. She has been a practising Reiki Master since 2009. She has served as Chief of Staff and Coach at UN Women USA, San Francisco Bay Area Chapter, and as a hospice volunteer at Kaiser Permanente in Redwood City, California. She has served as a Heartfulness Trainer in Suva, Fiji.

## Emotions as loyal messengers

Emotions are messengers, bringing us information about our internal state. For example, grief tells us we have loved deeply and hold attachments to that which is lost. Also, emotions are loyal as they come with good reason and a valid message. We do not grieve, experience joy or become angry without reason. Our task is to pay attention to the emotions and their communication. In order to do this effectively, we cannot deny, ignore, avoid or suppress emotions. Instead, we can seek to understand their messages.

Anger is a powerful messenger; it typically delivers a warning about the violation of a boundary, a disappointment around an expectation or the activation of triggers from trauma. While other emotions may feel like rivers in which we can be carried away, anger resembles the rapids in a stream.[36] Anger happens quickly, and we tumble into its powerful current. However, if we take the time to understand it properly, anger is a valuable tool to honour our boundaries in loving ways, release expectations and, ultimately, heal ourselves.

[36] This analogy is taken from the book *Sculpting Positivity: Daily Inspirations from the show 'Mornings with Marilyn.'* https://amzn.to/2T3NMJw

## Childhood trauma and its triggers

There are several distinct ways we may experience anger. For instance, we may become angry the moment someone does something that triggers us. Although anger happens the moment the trigger is activated, the source of the anger is often in the past. Triggers are like landmines – you never know when you might step on one – and they can be gravely dangerous. The landscape may look harmless to someone traversing it, but our trauma lies just below the surface. One wrong step from them, and we explode.

Anger and its triggers are often a sign of trauma, which is a lasting set of effects from negative or adverse childhood experiences (ACEs).[37] [38] Childhood trauma has lingering impacts on our adult lives in a variety of ways, including anxiety, depression, health problems, violence, and difficulties managing relationships.[39]

Let's look at an example of anger and childhood trauma. Ravi is short and grew up being bullied and called names. In particular, he was teased and humiliated using the label 'wimp.' Ravi has not taken the time to release the pent-up

[37] National Centre for Excellence for Complex Trauma. What is Childhood Trauma? https://www.blueknot.org.au/Resources/Information/Understanding-abuse-and-trauma/What-is-childhood-trauma

[38] The CDC's definition of ACEs: https://www.cdc.gov/violenceprevention/childabuseandneglect/aces/fastfact.html

[39] Copeland WE, Shanahan L, Hinesley J, et al. Association of Childhood Trauma Exposure With Adult Psychiatric Disorders and Functional Outcomes. *JAMA Netw Open*. 2018;1(7):e184493. doi:10.1001/jamanetworkopen.2018.4493

anger and humiliation from this childhood experience; it lies buried beneath the surface of his disposition.

Fast-forward 30 years and Ravi is in a board meeting. His team leader is lambasting him for not taking a calculated risk to land a million-dollar advertising client. As Ravi walks out of the conference room, a co-worker jokingly calls him a wimp, saying he would have taken the risk. Before he realizes what's happening, Ravi has pinned his colleague by the collar to the wall and is threatening him in a low and dangerous tone. The colleague is shocked and scared by this sudden move. Another colleague breaks them up, and Ravi heads to the restroom to splash some cold water on his face and ponder what just happened.

The word 'wimp' triggered old anger Ravi was still holding inside, and it readily exploded into action. In order to release the suppressed anger in healthy ways, Ravi might need to undergo psychotherapy, alternative healing, coaching or another type of practice to let the anger go for good. The message Ravi's anger is bringing him is about his inner child's unresolved trauma: 'Please protect and heal little Ravi. Help him to feel his true worth. Help him feel confident and safe.' This is an essential message that Ravi needs to heed.

## Anger masks fear

Another way anger shows up in our lives is through the way we are conditioned to hold emotions inside. Men are especially raised this way: it's labeled weak to show emotions, so they learn to bottle them up. When anger begins to accumulate from everyday interactions, they are vented on those who may have nothing to do with the cause of the anger in the first place. If we look deeper, we find anger masking fear.

The classic example is when a person in a stressful profession, perhaps a criminal lawyer, comes home from work. Jeff is quiet and brooding. An innocuous comment from his spouse Amy about whether he wants dinner now or later sparks a rant about wanting to be left alone. After a bitter and vicious tirade, Jeff may be rebuked by Amy or left alone. In most cases, Jeff cools off and after some time apologizes to Amy, citing work pressure as the source of his dark moods. Depending on how long this habit has been going on, Amy may feel like a punching bag for Jeff's frustration, and she begins to develop anger and resentment of her own. If this happens, then anger creates a chain reaction of more anger.

A lack of healthy ways to release anger – such as speaking to a friend or counsellor, exercising or meditating – results in inappropriate ways of venting anger on loved ones. What is Jeff's anger telling him? Perhaps, 'You're afraid of failing and appearing weak. You're holding too much inside. Please deal with this fear, which is showing up as anger, before you destroy your relationship with Amy and ruin your work prospects.'

## Anger and illness

Holding on to anger has adverse effects, not only on relationships at work and at home, but also on our bodies. Research suggests that chronic physical pain is related to trauma, and that we tend to relive our trauma when stressed.[40] In Eastern medicine, including Chinese medicine[41] and Ayurveda[42], anger is associated with the liver.

Also, anger manifests in the body as heat. Therefore, these healing traditions prescribe cooling foods such as coconut and the herb Shatavari, and staying away from pungent foods like garlic and chilies, as they did for me. I am releasing suppressed rage through my feet, which crack open, peel, and itch. This has been going on for four years.

As I began the journey to understand the confusing condition of my feet, which conventional doctors failed to diagnose except to say it was an autoimmune issue, I learned a lot about anger. Five alternative practitioners independently diagnosed it the same way: my body is releasing rage from abuse when I was a little child. These practitioners include two acupuncturists, a shaman, an acupressure and Chinese medicine expert, and a Vedic astrologer and Ayurveda specialist.

My anger wasn't being expressed through emotions; it was remembered by my body, so it had to be released at the physical level. Anger brought me this message: 'You were too young to process what happened to you emotionally,

[40] Susanne Babbel MFT, PhD. 2010. The Connections Between Emotional Stress, Trauma and Physical Pain: Chronic pain can be caused by trauma and stress. *Psychology Today*. https://www.psychologytoday.com/intl/blog/somatic-psychology/201004/the-connections-between-emotional-stress-trauma-and-physical-pain

[41] Cathy Wong. 2020. *Emotions in Traditional Chinese Medicine*

https://www.verywellmind.com/emotions-in-traditional-chinese-medicine-88196

[42] Bess O'Connor. 2015. 7 ways to tame anger with Ayurveda. https://spiritualityhealth.com/articles/2015/04/17/7-ways-tame-anger-ayurveda

but your body remembers, and you must allow the release to happen. This rage must make its way out of you. Be kind to yourself and be patient.'

Realising this, I began to focus on being a non-judgmental friend to myself in this difficult process of release. I forgave those who abused me, to the extent I could figure out their identities. As I released trauma, practised self-love, and forgave, my feet started to heal.

A former client, Gina, harbors anger against her mother for allowing her stepfather to abuse her on an ongoing basis while she was a young girl. One of the ways her anger shows up is through scars on her face and body. She picks at them – which is a sign of trauma – and the scars deepen and worsen. As someone who also has many scars and who used to pick at my face and feel ugly, I was able to empathise with her. She chose me as her coach because I understood what it's like to be abused.

I explained to Gina the importance of self-love, which helps us release self-harming habits. I will return to self-love later, after we look at some more examples of how anger brings us messages. In Gina's case, her anger was bringing her an important message: 'This abuse has been going on for so long that it's making you feel dirty, unlovable, and ugly. You're manifesting that by picking at your scars. Please face the underlying issue – you're angry with your mother and stepfather.'

How might Gina face this and release her anger? How might she also separate herself from her stepfather and mother? Gina's task was to stand up for herself, and, with coaching, she was able to move out and live separately from her family. She is currently releasing her anger and having compassion for herself, her mother, and her stepfather.

## Trauma, abuse, and revenge

Sometimes anger appears in the form of revenge. Another client, Kate, was molested as a teenager by one of her siblings. She felt helpless and resolved to run away from home. Eventually this came about when she went away to school. Her suppressed anger appeared in the form of holding grudges and desiring revenge against her brother and anyone else who harmed her emotionally throughout her life. Like me, she also experienced trauma in the form of large cracks on her feet.

When I began working with Kate, I realised that despite being a warm, loving, and compassionate human being, she would also harbour feelings of anger and revenge for years at a time. Kate suffered from a host of lifestyle risk factors, including diabetes, hypertension, and multiple autoimmune conditions, which affected her feet, hands, and hair.

We worked on exploring the feelings of revenge together, and she realised that she was holding on to the abuse by her brother, other family members, and colleagues over the years. Through five years of energy healing, meditation, life coaching, and a course on self-love, Kate was able to reverse her lifestyle risk factors, and realise that those who mistreated her had likely been abused too. Her sibling had already passed away, but she was able to forgive him and move on with her life. She was also able to dissolve her anger and allow her compassionate heart to lead the way. Kate's anger and revenge brought this message: 'You feel like you were a victim because you were. Empower yourself and remember who you are. Heal this old anger. Forgive and release it. Become love.' Kate listened to the message, acted upon it, finding liberation and joy.

Trauma from abuse – physical, sexual, emotional, and verbal – is a common cause of anger. One instance of extreme rage illustrates just how powerful anger can be when we don't heed its message. A former client, Bill, was raped as a young boy. We worked on releasing his fears and the tendency to hide from his life's calling. With coaching that included guided meditations, affirmations, and tailored exercises to build confidence toward launching his new career, Bill began to thrive.

However, a pattern soon emerged: Bill's anger would erupt without warning when he felt threatened. Bill was unstable but you wouldn't know it unless you witnessed one of these vicious anger outbursts. Because I worked closely with him, I became the target of several of his verbal lashings. The important characteristic of Bill's anger pattern was that it was completely subconscious. He had developed a blind spot with regard to how destructive his anger could be to its target. He simply didn't believe it when I explained to him what he was doing. He would show up the day after verbally attacking my family and me, as if nothing had transpired. He wanted to move on with our work. I had to stop working with Bill because he refused to acknowledge that his anger was harmful.

Bill's anger was bringing him this message: 'Anger has become a dangerous part of you. You are out to destroy people whenever you feel threatened. You won't acknowledge this, but you're self-sabotaging your relationships and career with this level of deeply held anger. Do something about it. Try to see it. This anger must be acknowledged and healed.'

Underneath the anger is Bill's deep pain and insecurity at being violated and the fear of it happening again. He subconsciously acts out to stop anything he perceives as more pain, but in the process he also reacts to harmless comments, hurting the people who are most able to support and help him. This self-sabotage is one of the signals of trauma and a lack of self-love.[43]

During trauma coaching work, I have encountered other examples of anger in people from different backgrounds and different countries that are identical to Bill's rage. For instance, Sandy refuses to give up her anger pattern; it's part of her way of interacting with co-workers and collaborators. She continues to destroy their confidence and self-esteem, and any attempt to point this out is met with blaming others. Sandy will simply say, 'If you don't like it, leave. You're the one who is creating the problem.' Louise is a cancer survivor with deep anger and guilt. She explodes with rage and then carries on as though nothing has happened. Any attempt to observe that she is holding on to

[43] For more on self-sabotage, see *The Path to Romantic Success: What You Won't Learn in School or at Home about True Love*. https://amzn.to/2VtjBgr

anger is met with more rage and the accusation that no one understands her.

Sadly, in such cases, the person is subconsciously suspicious of love, because they did not receive it as a child. Instead of love, they received abuse, so anger has become a familiar way of life and a cemented habit. Sabotage and suffering plague these people because they aren't able to let go of the painful but familiar past, so they keep recreating that past with suppressed anger, which masks fear.

## Practices for self-love and compassion

Anger is a powerful force in our lives. How we deal with anger or neglect it, can influence and even dictate how we develop as individuals, how well we function in relationships at home and at work, how effectively we manage our careers, and ultimately how well we can love ourselves and others.

The foundation of all love is self-love. When we create the habit of unconditionally loving ourselves just as we are, it gives us the courage and ability to go within and be present with our trauma. Without self-love, we might become overwhelmed, depressed, apathetic or cynical about the traumas we have faced.

It helps to have a good coach or guide who can create a safe and loving space in which to model self-love. Once we truly love ourselves, we can go into our trauma and work on it. Anger is a reliable messenger about the trauma that is still inside us. Using anger as a helpful tool, we can investigate our trauma and begin to release it. As we release trauma and its loyal symptom, anger, we begin to return to our original and true self with all our creativity, wonder, curiosity, joy, and love. Of course, we cannot restore the innocence of who we were before the trauma happened, but we can do even better: we can become our authentic selves bolstered with the learning we gain from healing that trauma.

Cultivating self-love also helps us to set healthy boundaries to avoid further abusive situations. Self-love means no longer accepting abusive behavior, because you love and respect yourself. If you truly and unconditionally love someone else, and they are abusive, it means that while you still love them you set boundaries with them to stop the harm. If they are abusing a child, for instance, you must intervene. When this intervention doesn't happen, as in Gina's case, it is likely that her mother was also abused, because she has low confidence, self-esteem, and courage, which has led to her inability to protect her own child. If others are causing harm to you, you must set boundaries for your own safety. Boundaries are a trustworthy sign of a healthy level of self-love.

In addition to self-love, contemplative tools such as meditation, yoga, journaling, and reflection are crucial for self-healing. When we meditate and journal regularly, we notice the signals of trauma, including anger, and can handle them with more detachment, becoming more discerning and compassionate.

With consistent contemplative practice, we will reach the other side of anger's message – self-love. It's now possible to cultivate spaciousness in all our interactions and have compassion for others, because we realise we all have trauma. When anger is triggered, we have mental and emotional space in which to place it, examine it, listen to its message, and respond with love and compassion for others and ourselves. Instead of getting carried away by anger's speedy current, we learn to float in a bubble of observation and lightness of being. In that bubble, we are protected from reactivity through mindfulness of our feelings, and we can respond with calmness, compassion, and authenticity.

Interestingly, people with deep rage often find it difficult to meditate; they don't trust contemplative techniques because being present with their own mind is very uncomfortable. Often the meditation technique is blamed as being ineffective. Extra work is needed to help them find ways to trust and open up to regulating their minds and releasing their anger.

Eventually, through consistent contemplative practices, we develop appreciation for anger and other emotions. All emotions are messengers, bringing us vital information about where trauma lurks and where healing is needed. As we restore ourselves and begin to extend our love from ourselves to other people, and to all of life, we begin to see that we are all one. We realise that our collective journey is the same, with different details of misfortune, abuse, trauma, and healing. Compassion begins to rule our lives. We awaken to the fact that anger has always been an emissary, bringing us news of our true nature, love. Our collective journey is about becoming love, and anger provides strategic directions and important messages for how to achieve and maintain our true nature through pattern recognition and trauma healing.

## *Suggestions*

Emotions are messengers about your internal state. They are there for good reason. Pay attention to what they are telling you. Anger is a powerful and volatile messenger.

While anger is triggered in the present, the source of the anger is often in the past.

Anger can mask other emotions, like fear, and it can lead to other emotions, like resentment.

Anger that has not been released is remembered in your body. It takes time to release it, so be kind to yourself and patient.

Find ways to forgive others, release trauma and practise self-love.

Practices:

- Find a capable guide or coach who can create a safe and loving space in which to model self-love.
- Use anger as a helpful tool to investigate trauma and release it.
- Meditation, yoga, journaling and reflection are crucial for self-healing.

# Expressing and Evolving Emotions

VICTOR KANNAN

## About Victor Kannan

Victor has a master's degree in Economics and has held several senior executive positions in Corporate America since the 1980s. He is also a certified meditation trainer in the Heartfulness Meditation system.

He lives in Atlanta Georgia with his wife, and their daughter lives in California. As an independent thinker, he writes frequently for various magazines and blog sites. His favourite topics are self-development, spirituality, and meditation.

## My story

I grew up in a very large family. My mother was the eldest of sixteen siblings. Between my mother's and father's families, we have more than fifty cousins and one hundred nieces and nephews. I grew up attending the many events that happen in a large family – not just birthdays, but also events like weddings, engagements, religious festivals, etc. For us children, it was a time of fun and play, to get together, run around, eat, receive gifts, and leave. I am also the youngest of six siblings.

Recollecting my early years, I remember that I had not seen anyone in my family, including my father, getting angry. I grew up not knowing how to express anger.

Having been on the move from my early twenties, and assuming responsibilities that seemed beyond my capacity, I realised I did not have many friends. I took my responsibilities to heart and tried to fulfil them to the best of my knowledge and abilities. I don't think I came across any situation that warranted anger until my adult years. When those situations arose, and in the absence of not knowing how to get angry, I was frustrated and worried. I withdrew internally looking for someone to understand me.

I began to encounter difficult situations during my thirties, which were at odds with my understanding. My reactions to these situations and circumstances were shock, surprise, and sadness, instead of anger and expressiveness. As I did not know how to get angry, I had a lot of quiet frustration and sleepless nights, thinking how I should respond. Having grown up emotionally unchallenged, I was unable to relate to emotional turbulence.

When I left home because of career opportunities, I realised that I was an introvert. I also had a fear of public speaking. I began to see more heterogeneity in society and various ways of thinking. This kept me an introvert, along with a fear of socialising. I wonder if this fear also kept me from getting angry. I realised that when there is fear, anger remains suppressed. This could potentially be a terrible situation.

At the age of eleven, I tried to overcome my fear of the dark and loneliness by walking through the woods at night. I was determined to overcome that fear. Over time, however, I experienced the fear of heights, flying, driving, and ghosts. Most of these fears were overcome very consciously and very quickly. I had heard a motivational speaker explain FEAR as an acronym for False Evidence Appearing Real. Now, I can say much of my fear is gone. I am comfortable in my own skin irrespective of whom I am with.

There are different triggers for different people. After years of analysing myself, I have understood that I am triggered when my intentions are misunderstood or when someone takes advantage of my goodness or behaves unfairly in general. One fine morning in the spring of the late '90s, I woke up with these clear words in my heart: 'It is unfair to expect fairness.' This was a big revelation, and it reduced the complexity of misunderstanding. I realised that pent-up frustration erupts as anger when another person repeatedly accuses me while misunderstanding my intentions.

I learned the skill of getting angry over a decade or two. Does that seem strange to you, reader? How can it be a skill if it is a spontaneous reaction usually accompanied by unawareness and lack of control? When anger advances to rage, there is a neurological dissociation and loss of presence, and we tend to forget the sequence of events that caused the escalation. This also adversely affects our ability to introspect and to engineer changes in our temperament.

Frustration advancing into anger is a natural process of response to a situation that does not fit our psychological frame of mind. Dealing with it properly is of utmost importance. Excessive anger, rage, and neurological dissociation is as bad as being frozen without getting angry when a situation warrants it. Frozen energies of reaction cause trauma and takes decades of therapy. Uncontrolled rage creates more damage to both the self and the target of that anger. Many times, such rage creates irreversible damage to loved ones in families.

In recent years, it appears that my anger is being expressed in a purer fashion, without the complexity of fear. When I am angry with co-workers it is mainly due to dishonest behavior, and I try to set things right following my father's example of not publicly insulting or disrespecting. In this I use techniques akin to Chanakya's four *Neetis*, namely, request, reward, punish, injure.

When I recall a few instances of anger in recent years, they feel natural to me, though I feel very bad about getting angry at the persons concerned. I am frustrated with myself when I make stupid mistakes and comments, however, I introspect and visualise how to make things better. I think of how I could have avoided those situations to begin with. I dissect them to understand what triggered the anger and how to communicate without getting angry.

I have been practising Heartfulness since I was twenty-two. This has helped me evolve my emotions and their expression. It is critical to understand the difference between complexity and simplicity in these emotions. When two or more emotions are combined in varying intensities, it creates a solid complex set of emotions. When we loosen the knot of complexity, we arrive at pure emotion. Anger is akin to passion and passion is an expression of love. So, while this connection of anger with love is strange, it is critical to understand.

## The wisdom of sages

Lord Buddha said, 'Holding on to anger is like grasping a hot coal with the intent of throwing it at someone else; you are the one who gets burned.' As far as love is concerned, he taught us to 'Radiate boundless love towards the entire world – above, below, and across – unhindered, without ill will, without enmity.' Furthering that idea, he told his disciples to teach this triple truth to all: 'A generous heart, kind speech, and a life of service and compassion are the things which renew humanity.'

A saint who lived in 19th century India named Lalaji (Ram Chandra, 1873-1931) prescribed a simple and effective method to change the inner state and the relationship between two people who are at odds with each other. I have been practising this technique for the past five years. It is a visualisation to develop empathetic and compassionate sentiments in the heart toward someone who has hurt me or made me angry. Then, to send love-filled thoughts to that person. I use this whenever I face a tough situation at work or in the family, when I feel upset, angry or misunderstood. I experience a great inner change when I send love-filled thoughts to a person who made me angry. It shifts my consciousness, and I am lighter and clearer because of it. It helps me deal with those people who trigger my anger in day-to-day life, so that there is no holding onto the memory or situation. This sort of reset has improved my relationships enormously.

I have also learned that I need a good command over the vocabulary of various feelings and emotions, so that I can clearly express how I feel. I need a felt sense of understanding and appropriate association of words to such feelings. Then, I need to develop the ability to properly respond to the stimulus. Unfortunately, I didn't learn how to do this at school or college. The school of life is a very difficult and unpredictable one. It does not have a proper method laid out in a curriculum. It is left to our choices and circumstances. We need to change this paradigm and begin to live and learn consciously.

## Emotions and feelings

Today many psychologists talk about emotional intelligence. Daniel Goleman, the author, science journalist, and fellow from Harvard, has written several books about emotional intelligence, pioneering the aspect of learning the emotions of life and their expression. Dr. Goleman defines emotional intelligence as our ability to manage our emotions and feelings and learn how to appropriately express those feelings. Expressing our emotions is critical. According to Goleman, emotional intelligence plays a significant role in our success in the workplace as well as in social circles.

It is necessary to make a distinction between emotions and feelings, as we often use these two words interchangeably. I recall a story about the spiritual teacher Babuji (Ram Chandra 1899-1983) who was taking leave from his disciples after having spent a considerable amount of time with them. They had had a wonderful love-filled and serene time together, and the disciples were overcome by deep emotions, unable to control their weeping as their Guru was leaving them to be with another group far away. One of the older disciples asked Babuji why there was no reaction on his face in response to their sadness and weeping. Babuji replied that what they had was emotion and what he had were feelings for them.

Emotions, if not well understood and refined, don't evolve into feelings. One definition of emotions is that they are associated with visceral, visible, and audible bodily reactions. They are activated through neurotransmitters and hormones released by the body, brain, and the heart's response to them. The heart races and the body sweats.

There is also a dissociation that takes place during rage and enactments of anger, as a safety mechanism to preserve the rest of the body's function. Eventually, however, the body gives up if we pursue emotional outbursts without any self-awareness or self-regulation.

Experience has taught me that feelings are our understanding of the experience of these emotional reactions, however mild or acute they may be. For this to happen, we need to be taught to recognise the various emotions we experience and develop appropriate transformational strategies to convert them into feelings and conscious positive action.

In the interest of clarity and understanding, we can define emotions as the first reaction to a stimulus, for example, a spontaneous flight, fight or freeze response. In contrast, feelings are deeper, subtler, and less volatile. Feelings unexpressed may lead to emotionally frozen energy, having deleterious mental and behavioral consequences. Hence, once emotions are transformed into feelings, then, feelings are best expressed in a conscious and productive manner.

How can we recognise the emotions we have? Emotions are recognised when acted upon, because there is a person, event or a thing in front of us. Emotions can also be defined as a certain energy in motion. Thought energy is converted into kinetic energy and passed on to the people and things around us. For example, a negative emotion may result in yelling, screaming, crying or even throwing things. It crashes parties and events, insults loved ones, and creates a scene. The perpetrator gets attention, including getting beaten up at times. It is a negative spiral with no good immediate outcome.

Such an extreme energy in motion eventually triggers circuit breakers, creating the natural mechanism to put a stop to the energy in motion. Then the quiet that follows the storm provides an opportunity for damage assessment and rehabilitation. If we are taught to recognise the ill effects of such emotions, and learn to manage them, then we will be moving toward feelings about the people, events and things that happen around us.

Feelings, too, may make us moody. When we have feelings, we have to figure out what to do as a result of those feelings. Emotional intelligence is so much more than no longer being an emotional wreck; it is about becoming an intelligent feeler. So, the transformation continues while we master our emotions and then transform them into positive feelings.

This transformation of a negative emotion into a positive feeling is a very satisfying journey. It inspires us to explore possibilities. It motivates us to embark upon a self-transformational journey, like the stories of people who have gone through the deep end only to scale the lofty heights of the two majestic mountains of peace and calmness. Here we find focus, self-awareness, and self-control. We easily get into flow and performance. We feel the joy of life. When we are joyful, we are generous rather than jealous; we are loving and kind rather than hateful and vengeful; we feel safe rather than insecure.

## Moving from complex to simple emotions

Another thing I have learned over the years is that our emotions become more complex as one primary emotion is mixed with other emotions. For example, when anger and fear combine it makes a terrible combination. Fear promotes prejudice. Now we have a really complex bundle. When anger erupts it could be triggered because of fear or prejudgment of a person or an event. The more complex the base of emotions, the more rapid the reaction becomes. So, it is important to recognise this phenomenon and begin to work on loosening the complexities, simplifying the emotions, and then rewriting them.

In a nutshell, to evolve and transform, we need to simplify and purify our emotions into feelings. This is a process of evolution of mind or consciousness. We move from complexity to simplicity, from negativity to positivity, from the complex of anger, jealousy, insecurity, and fear to simple anger to unconditional love.

## What helps us do this?

Fortunately, when I was twenty-two, I met a colleague who became a lifelong fellow traveler on the self-transformation journey. He talked me into meditating, and I had nothing to lose. I had been a skeptic since the age of seventeen, but I knew that I didn't know a lot of things or understand many things around me, so I kept an open mind along with a dose of healthy skepticism.

The very first meditation aroused curiosity, and after forty years I am still meditating; it helps me enormously on a daily basis. Now I understand how to recognise emotions and feelings and what tools to use to manage them.

## The positive rewriting of emotions

One such tool is as simple as the positive rewriting of emotions. When I feel frustrated or angry with some of my team members or colleagues, I send them love-filled vibrations. I sit with eyes closed and from the safety and comfort of my space I sincerely feel love for those people. This transforms my inner condition and also has a mystical and magical effect on the people and the circumstances. I have seen this happen repeatedly. While new situations keep arising as we live through our life fully, we become adept in using these tools and techniques to influence situations so that we can manage them and nurture them into a positive space.

Introspection, visualisation, meditation, and positive rewriting can change the emotional scale of our lives. If the negative effects of past emotional reactions are stored in the body-mind complex, there are several meditative detox practices that help in cleaning away the body memories and impressions of those situations so that we can reset.

Life has to be lived, challenges overcome, life's purpose achieved, meaning found, so that ultimately we can transcend this life peacefully to whatever may await us next. We can waste our life in negative emotions like anger and frozen emotions like fear or we can find a way to stay inspired, positive, and loving.

## Suggestions

Become an intelligent feeler. Learn to express how you feel, and develop a deep understanding of the words needed to communicate your emotions and feelings.

Radiate boundless love through a generous heart, kind speech, and a life of service and compassion.

Simplify your emotions. For example, fear can suppress or compound anger. Move from complex emotional combinations to simple emotions to feelings. Practise heart-based meditation to bring about this transform.

Don't expect fairness.

When excessive anger leads to rage it can cause neurological dissociation, creating frozen energy and causing trauma.

Practices:

- Introspect and then visualise how to make things better. Ask yourself how you can avoid those situations in future.
- Positively rewrite your emotions. For example, Lalaji's simple visualisation practice to develop positivity toward someone who has hurt you or made you angry. It involves sending love-filled thoughts.

# The Heart's Alchemy

ELIZABETH DENLEY

## About Elizabeth Denley

Elizabeth has been involved in developing value-based education and training programs for schools and colleges in India, Australia, Fiji, Europe, Africa, and North America for the last 25 years, and coordinated the development of the Heartfulness Education Programs for schools. She is a trained facilitator, developing, coordinating, and facilitating interactive programs in communication, life skills, consciousness, and personal development.

Elizabeth has been a certified Heartfulness trainer for over 30 years, and is actively involved in content development for Heartfulness, including as the founding editor-in-chief of Heartfulness Magazine. She has also delivered many online and in-person programs and training courses around the world. Elizabeth holds a Ph.D. in Biological Sciences, and has worked in research in ecology, mental health, and education in Australia, U.S.A., the Philippines, and India.

## My story

For as long as I can remember it has been natural to love; not surprising as it is the female imperative, and all about connection. But anger has been a different journey. When I was small, if things were not right, I would feel a friction in the heart, turbulent vibrations. My awareness of the inner state was quite scientific. I believe that all children naturally do this – they observe.

Over time, I discovered that anger became complicated when thoughts and emotions created an entanglement in those vibrations. Then it could blow up into an ocean storm within, and affect my whole being. I always knew that the friction occurred first in my energy field of consciousness, and that then triggered a physiological response. It was never the other way round.

Modern psychologists would say that my discomfort with anger is rooted in early trauma, and that is true in one sense, but I have never looked at life that way. It is more useful to explore the energy and vibrations around different inner states. What are they trying to tell me?

Emotions are interpretations of those inner vibrations – our reactions and responses to life. They are sometimes painful, sometimes pleasurable, sometimes neither. They are always there to help, warn, and guide toward the next step in life's journey. Problems arose only when I became stuck in patterns that did not lead toward resolution and letting go.

I also learned that friction in the heart does not only happen with anger – any emotion can create turbulence, like grief, disappointment, fear, worry, guilt, excitement, and passion. Looking back, anger was often entangled with many other emotions, creating a compound emotion.

In early childhood I used two words to describe these inner states of being: 'rough' and 'smooth.' As an adult, those words became 'turbulent' and 'still.' Of course, there are many nuances within those states, and it is really a spectrum from utter stillness to extreme turbulence, like we see in the ocean. In that worldview, anger was fiery turbulence, but the fiery part was often held inside and mixed with other elements, especially the water element. That led to sadness.

When I first read the books of Ram Chandra (Babuji), I was fascinated by his statement that passion (*kama*) and anger (*krodha*) are two emotions that cannot be destroyed. That meant to me that they serve an evolutionary and natural purpose in our existence. So, I embarked on a journey to understand that purpose – how could passion and anger be transformed into their most noble expressions? I learned that they are both rooted in our evolutionary imperative, and interlinked through the element of fire and the third chakra within the Heart. Fire is the element of purification, ascension, and the ego, our identity.

## The heart's signature

I also learned that each of us has our own signature of the Heart – our personal interplay of the five elements of earth, ether, fire, water, and air, and the associated five chakras within the Heart Region. With that comes a unique signature of emotions, much like we have a unique set of fingerprints. Some of us are fiery, others earthy and grounded in our approach to life, but none of us has the exact same mix of these five elements. Our signature is unique, and that gives a unique fragrance and colourto our emotions, including anger and love.

Once the chakras in the Heart Region are purified of the past patterns of samskara, then we see these emotions in their unalloyed form. That happens through contemplative practice and results in an evolution of consciousness. But even then, the signature of each heart remains, as the subtlest colouring of personality. As a result, there is no 'one size fits all' stereotype for either anger or love.

In order to dive to a deeper level of understanding of both emotions, I would like to explore the fire element and the third chakra of the heart. This is where we really begin to uncover the true nature of love and anger, and where the alchemical work of transforming passion and anger into pure emotions happens.

## Passion, love, shadow work, and enlightenment

But first, what has passion got to do with love? Passion is one aspect of love. In some languages there are many words for 'love,' like in Russian and Sanskrit. English expresses the nuances of love differently, using adjectives to qualify love, for example, motherly love, romantic love, filial love, spiritual love, friendly love, brotherly love, etc. whereas in Russian and Sanskrit, the varieties of love have been assigned different nouns. Language reflects culture – we approach love with different cultural consciousnesses, but either way, we all agree that love has many dimensions.

One expression of love is passion, through the fire element. As a pure energy, passion is inspirational; it propels us toward someone or something, connecting us with that person or thing. Passion in the physical body is often sensual, leading to lovemaking for procreation and human bonding. Passion in the mental body is associated with principles, ideals, vision, and the motivation needed to excel in any endeavor. Passion in the realm of feelings creates interest, enthusiasm, and romantic love. When the fiery energy of passion is expressed spiritually, it propels us toward God. It is associated with devotion, creativity and connection, it transmutes from passion to compassion as we grow beyond self-interest, and it propels us to great heights, both in worldly and spiritual endeavors. Passion is aspirational. It creates restlessness, longing, and the fuel we need to succeed. It is a function of our identity, the 'I' that wants to evolve. That identity is known as the ego, one of the aspects of the mind.

The ego needs a lot of refining, if it is not to inflate, distort, and become what Carl Jung calls the 'shadow.' In fact, in Western psychology, the process of evolution of consciousness is all about 'shadow work' – about bringing to light those parts of ourselves that are hidden in the subconscious, which we prefer not to see. The aim is to integrate them into our being.

The same is true in the Eastern tradition of Yoga, and in other spiritual traditions. In fact, Yoga offers us the most sophisticated system of psychology I have discovered in all my searches so far. Here is what one yogi had to say about 'shadow work' – he was called Ram Chandra (Lalaji). This is from a text written at the beginning of the 20th century, where he is talking about the various layers or coverings of the human being:

> The fourth covering is the region of the intellect, which is the element involved in making decisions. The mind proposes, and the element which confirms the proposal is known as *buddhi*, the intellect. With the help of the intellect, an opportunity is available to see the reflection of Reality, to a certain extent.
>
> But this covering, being subtle like the mind, eludes and deceives at times. Those who approach it begin to get the power of performing miracles and powers of many kinds. In this case, those who tread the path of the Divine may be so badly deceived that they do not get a chance to rise back to the right stage easily. It is therefore essential to remove this covering with great care.

> The amorous playfulness of the intellect is an extremely complicated affair. And the shadow of the intellect is the ego. Those under the influence of ego fall down. Those who have not actually seen this covering of intellect, but have only gone near to it, come under the shadow of ego. They argue uselessly in favourof their opinions and never care for truth or reality. They fall and become entangled in the net of rebirths. It is therefore important and necessary to be cautious about the ego.

Here Lalaji shares the importance of shining a light on the identities the ego creates when they are hidden in the shadow of the subconscious.

But then, Lalaji's associate, Babuji, writes, 'In my opinion, the mind and the ego are the only two things in man, the best and the most useful. In fact, ego refers to the real Being, and mind searches it out. Really, we have to learn the proper utilisation of everything in man. There must not be misuse of anything. That is humanity in the true sense.'

Why this apparent paradox? It requires understanding the process of refining the ego to become a friend not an enemy, because the ego is integrally associated with the emotions of anger and love.

That process involves shining a light into the shadows of the subconscious, and removing the complexities, purifying the canvas of consciousness, so the light can shine through. It is not an accident that we meditate on the source of light that is at the centre of our being. It illuminates us from the inside out, so that the light radiates and permeates through all the layers to the very periphery of our existence. Babuji describes it as 'light without luminosity.' That process is enlightenment.

## Making friends with anger

For much of my life, the fiery emotion of anger was drowned in watery feelings of sadness, disappointment, and disillusionment. I would feel alone and hurt, with a bursting heart, stuck in the pattern of being let down by people. I would shut off from the people who disappointed or hurt me as a defense. I didn't feel angry toward them – just disillusioned and wounded. I always knew they were doing the best they could, and that their behavior wasn't centred around me. I could accept the imperfections and continue to love, but I could not process the inner heartbreak.

Becoming aware of this pattern and removing the layers of its persistent and subtle influence on my psyche, has been a psychological liberation. The inner friction of anger is no longer heavy. Instead, it is a catalyst to explore what needs to change, opening a whole new realm of possibilities. These days, that inner friction is less frequent and less intense; it has gone from heavy to lighter to subtler. I am able to hold greater awareness, and explore what needs to change within.

## Working with anger

This transformation is the direct result of an ongoing spiritual practice.[44] Anger is now a tool for evolution. When I observe friction in the heart, it is a reason for inquiry: What is causing this? Do I need to let go of anything? What needs to change? What intentions can I create for change? What habits and tendencies can I work upon? It is not that I feel less than before; in fact, there is greater sensitivity.

But I don't believe for one minute that self-awareness and introspection are responsible for the transformation that has occurred. They are the outcome. The inner spiritual work happens at a much deeper level, in the subconscious, removing the programmed cognates at the vibrational level – the samskaras. As they are removed, the associated feelings and habits often rise into consciousness, although sometimes a negative habit just remarkably disappears, like magic!

This process is supported by two complementary yogic techniques: the Transmission and Cleaning. Effectively, Cleaning is spiritual surgery, removing blockages and complexities from the canvas of consciousness, and infusing life-transforming Transmission to replenish and nourish it. These techniques bypass the mental approach, purifying the vibrational patterns in the field of consciousness directly.

[44] I have been a Heartfulness practitioner for over 30 years.

As an example, one day I had an experience during a meditation session, and wrote to Daaji:
'Today was very challenging. I could not meditate well this morning because of a disturbed condition due to a series of unfortunate events. But then something marvelous happened. In the evening, I requested a meditation session from a trainer and once I closed my eyes I experienced the awareness of fire, like a column up the centre of my system, rising upwards. It was a clear burning, leading to a clarity that was laser-like.

'While the experiences of the day were being cleaned, there was no mental analysis. Only purification and incredible clarity. Eventually the column of fire became white, and I understood the white colourof the third chakra in a new way. It then became transparent yet still highly charged. Powerless power. This essence of anger had no emotion and no force. The day's disappointments and frustrations were purified by fire. Everything in the furnace – all the characters in the drama. I am not able to explain it well in words.'

Daaji's reply was, 'Fire transforms anger. It can also burn all the other unnecessary impediments, including ego.'
There was no need for a mental analysis of the situation, nor any post-mortem of who did what. Everything was burnt off during this one meditation session.

This inner work is the spiritual journey, which starts at the first chakra of the Heart Region and continues through the five chakras of the Heart, before carrying onward to other regions. When I arrived at the third chakra I started to understand more about the true nature and purpose of anger and love, and how they play out in our evolution.

Both these emotions have continued to mature and refine further over time, but the third chakra remains the reference point for the refinement of love and anger, and the element of fire continues to fulfil its role of purifying while there is anything to be burnt off.

## The alchemy of love and anger

For me, the alchemy of love and anger is the purification and igniting of inspiration, aspiration, motivation, creativity, enthusiasm, and the removal of blockages to the ascension to higher realms.

It is not surprising that there is so much mythology around the element of fire in every culture: the phoenix rising from the ashes, the story of Prometheus in Greek mythology, and the deities of fire like Agni, Ra, Vulcan, Vesta, and Logi. Fire is fundamental to our existence and it always takes us out of our comfort zone.

The first and second chakras of the Heart provide the support and stability for us to experience the fire element at the third chakra. The first chakra is associated with the element earth, and the feeling of contentment that comes when we let go of worldly desires. The heart is our midpoint, and when this first chakra is purified and awakened we have a stable base from which to journey. The second chakra introduces us to the experience of the soul and the element of ether. We glimpse what it feels like to be liberated from the physical plane of matter. We become immersed in the peace and stillness of the soul. We learn to integrate the experience of being a soul in a physical body as these two chakras together form a foundation.

Then, when we journey to the third chakra, we start to master the divine emotions of love and anger. Fire is volatile and transformative. At times it is painful and at other times ecstatic. It dislodges the ego in both directions, like elastic stretching and bouncing back until we let go of both. Without this process, we would not move forward. Love and anger are the tools that help us on that journey, but neither are the endpoint. They eventually fade to the subtlest forms of themselves. When we remain centred in the heart, the experience of this volatile essence is most natural. It is alchemical, like the ancient symbolism of the phoenix rising out of the ashes. How beautifully we are made! How astounding it is that we have the conscious awareness to experience this magical journey that is the gift of our human destiny!

## Suggestions

Anger starts as a frictional vibration in the heart. It gets stuck when thoughts and emotions create entanglements in that vibration and reinforce it. Children know how to read those vibrations. Try to remember back to when you did that naturally, and ask yourself, 'What are the vibrations telling me?'

Anger can never be destroyed. It has an evolutionary purpose.

Anger and love are interlinked through the element of fire, the third chakra of the Heart, and the mental function of ego. They propel us forward, refining the ego, shining light on the subconscious and removing the shadow-self of subconscious patterns. Fire takes us out of our comfort zone.

While anger is a fiery emotion, when it is mixed with other elements like water, it creates compound emotions. We all have our own emotional signature giving a unique colourto anger and love. Once the heart is purified through meditation practices, we see emotions in their unalloyed form.

Practices:

- Make friends with anger. Let it be a catalyst for change and new possibilities.
- Ask: What is causing this? Do I need to let go of anything? What needs to change? What intentions can I create for change? What habits and tendencies can I work upon?

# Understanding Love

DAAJI

## From me to we to thou

At the beginning of this book, we discussed the idea that most of us struggle with anger. I would also say that most of us struggle with love. Whether we feel love for a partner, children, friends, strangers, a spiritual teacher or God, there is always a journey with twists and turns. It is just as Lysander says in Shakespeare's *A Midsummer Night's Dream,* 'The course of true love never did run smooth.' And why is that? Because when we truly love we lose our individuality: we become love itself. Our own personal needs and desires are subsumed in something much grander than the individual 'I.' During that process, first 'we' takes precedence over 'I,' and eventually 'thou' takes precedence over 'we.' Stories of true love abound in every culture, and always love triumphs when the lover gives themselves totally to the beloved. Where does that then lead?

There is a wonderful short story by the American writer, O. Henry, called *The Gift of the Magi,* in which Jim and Della are very poor and very much in love. Each has a most treasured possession – Della's beautiful long hair and Jim's gold watch. One Christmas, they both secretly decide to sell these treasures so that they can buy presents for the other. Della cuts and sells her hair so that she can buy a chain for Jim's gold watch, and Jim sells his watch so that he can buy beautiful combs for Della's beautiful long hair. Each sells the most valuable thing they own to buy a gift for the other. For Jim and Della there is only 'thou.'

There is another story about Lord Krishna having a headache. The sage Narada asks Krishna how the headache can be removed, and Krishna replies, 'Bring me the dust from the feet of a true devotee.' Narada sets off to find a devotee, but most of Lord Krishna's devotees are reluctant to comply, because they know that if the dust from their feet touches the Lord's head it will be such a blasphemy that they go to hell. None of them will accept this fate. Finally, Narada visits the gopis, who have already heard of the Lord's request. He finds them collecting the dust from their feet to ease their Lord's headache.
He asks, 'Aren't you scared that you will go to hell?'
They reply, 'If we can give relief and comfort to our Lord even for a moment, we are ready to suffer in hell forever!'
Such was their love. Again, only 'thou.'

## What is love?

Just as anger originates in the subtle energetic body, which then affects the physical body, so love originates beyond the physical body in the inner depths of our being. When we speak of a loving heart, we don't mean the physical pumping organ, but something much subtler.

Love creates connection, love is the gravity of the soul – the weak force of attraction that holds everything together. Love is the source of enthusiasm for life itself, and the way we create osmosis with anyone or anything. Love allows us to resonate in vibrational compatibility. Love propels us toward the beloved. In fact, without love, whatever we do in life will be dry and mechanical, whereas when love is involved we will have a spring in our step and strive to improve and excel. 'It's love that makes the world go round,' in the words of W.S. Gilbert.

My first Guide, Babuji, once wrote about love in the following way:

> The love of a mother is very well known. The guru's love is less well known, and God's love is even less known. It is really no different from the love of the mother, who greatly cares for the safety of her child, even if the child misbehaves or hurts her. She always thinks of various means to keep the child happy and joyful. It is the same with the Guru, who is actually the spiritual mother ... with God as the father. The Guru always wants his spiritual child to make immense progress, which consequently induces God to look after the upbringing of the child, because the spiritual mother cares so much for the child.
>
> In this world there is no example of love greater than that of a mother for her child. You may question, 'How can a mother be compared to the Guru?' Just as the mother develops the child in her womb for a fixed period, the Guru does the same for us. You are brought up in his sphere of remembrance, fed by his energy, and your development takes place in his thought-current. When all these things are completed and it is no longer necessary to keep you in his womb of thought, you are delivered as his spiritual child. Where? The place of birth is the Brighter World. ... In Persian, this birthing is known as the process of initiation, and one who is initiated has completely

> surrendered himself. If a person has surrendered himself in the true sense, then it takes only seven months.

When I first met Babuji in 1977, a year after starting the Heartfulness practices, his utter simplicity amazed me. Just looking at him made me wonder how there could be such purity and simplicity in a person. His whole being radiated love. I could feel the Transmission flowing through him all the time. Even when he was silent, which was most of the time, there was always an inner communion; I was busy feeling his presence inside.

## How to become more loving?

We become more loving by purifying the subtle body, the energy field of the heart-mind. Through this process, we learn to regulate our thoughts, work on our patterns and fears, transcend our desires and emotional reactions, develop our decision-making ability, our generosity of heart, our inner strength, and our capacity to love. This happens through the practices of Meditation, Cleaning, and Prayer. These practices support love's gravity so that we orbit the Centre of our being, constantly in communion with the cause of our existence, the soul.

In that communion, love naturally radiates from every atom of our being, effortlessly, without the need for 'I.' There is no 'I' in true love. When a drop of water has merged in the ocean, does the drop remain to talk about itself? Identity is no longer needed.

Heartfulness focuses on the heart and love, and the first step is to purify and awaken the heart so that love for all of creation starts to flow. The second step is perhaps even more important – the gradual release of the ego's multiple identities, allowing consciousness to expand into more and more of the creation and beyond. Eventually all that is left is the Centre itself and its manifestation.

With this progression come the symptoms of love – compassion, kindness, understanding, acceptance, surrender, humility, and innocence.

## Transmission

When we speak of love, we must also speak of Transmission, as it is the utilisation of love for human transformation. Transmission removes the inner complexities of our energy field, cleaning and illuminating the spiritual centres or chakras. It is Transmission that removes the obstacles on our journey to the Centre. It makes meditation truly dynamic. It is the original divine essence, flowing from the Guide's heart into the hearts of seekers, just as a mother's love flows naturally to her children.

Transmission is not bound by physical laws. The moment we invoke Transmission it starts to flow, and we receive it wherever we are, instantaneously. The effect is that our attention flows inward to the Centre, so our whole system becomes highly stable, leading to lower and lower entropy. That Centre around which the vortex of our life exists is the soul.

Here is an analogy that may explain this better:

Imagine a beautiful flower in the garden. When you run past it, you don't appreciate its beauty; when you walk by it, you enjoy it more; when you stand in front of it, you appreciate its beauty to an even greater extent. When you are moving too fast, you miss out on many things.

Imagine, your mind is faster than any physical movement. When it moves rapidly from one thing to another, you miss out on the blossoming of the flower within you. You even miss out on the existence of the flower itself! That flower is the soul, and Transmission attracts you so deeply into the stillness within that your attention is drawn to that flower.

How can you look after it? Meditation is the way to look after it with so much love that it blossoms. Meditation centres the mind and helps it to be peaceful, matching the inner stillness of the sacred flower. You try to match that inner stillness, the essence of the soul, with the mind. That is the moment of Realisation – the perfect resonance of all your bodies with the innermost sacred flower, when you are whole.

Transmission *is* love, yet it also goes beyond love. On the inner journey, we are moving toward the Centre, the nothing-ness, so how will we be one with that Centre when we still have vibrations, even those of love? Transmission comes from the Centre and touches the Centre, so it must be the absolute essence of nothing-ness. It is indescribable.

We feel the effect of Transmission as relaxation of the body and stillness of the mind. Emotionally we move to a balanced 'zero' state within. Everything becomes quieter, and the vibrations all come to a standstill. We are able to evolve from whatever we are now to a clean canvas. Transmission is at the very heart of this transformative process.

We can say that Transmission is life-giving, but why would we need this when we already have a life force within us, the soul? Is the soul not sufficient for life? Imagine the analogy of trees during a drought in the hot summer months, when the leaves are wilting on the branches. The life-force is under stress, although the roots keep on absorbing whatever moisture and nutrients they can to survive. When the first rains come, the trees are renewed with freshness and vitality. Similarly, the moment we receive the first Transmission, there is new freshness in our existence. We receive it and we also unconsciously share it with others, as the heart is saturated with its essence. Having received Transmission, we distribute it, sharing the love.

Meditation with Transmission acts like a cane or crutch to support the expansion of consciousness into other dimensions. It helps us transcend from one level to another, soaring higher into superconsciousness and diving deeper into the subconscious depths of the mind. There are no limits to this expansion. Even the Universe is not enough when consciousness expands with this love.

Once we learn to absorb the meditative state we experience each morning during meditation, it deepens into constant remembrance, and our consciousness remains in contact with the Centre. Over time, this connection blossoms into love.

Heartfulness is all about love. It is a love story between the self and God, and it starts with the simple act of meditation. Meditation is the mother of constant remembrance, and constant remembrance is the mother of love. When we lead a life with love, everything is natural. We are not caught in the whirlpools of mental and emotional turbulence, so we remain balanced and calm within.

It is not that meditation gives us everything – meditation creates the inner condition, and the condition changes us. Our inner environment changes, faith develops, and acceptance follows. Acceptance leads to surrender and love, and we lose ourselves in the state of oneness.

## Emotional intelligence

The first things we observe during meditation are the emotions and feelings arising in the heart. These feelings and emotions affect our thinking process, especially through the limbic system of the mid-brain, once the initial impulse arises in the heart.

Many of us are not comfortable exploring how we feel, simply because we were not encouraged to do so when we were growing up, either at home or at school. There is so much talk today of emotional intelligence, including the heart-based qualities of compassion, empathy, resilience, love, courage and will, and these qualities emanate from the chakras of the heart. To improve our emotional intelligence, we need to work with the heart.

In the *Bhagavad Gita*, Lord Krishna mentions the qualities we need in order to cope with life's struggles. He uses an analogy: In life we are protected by noble qualities, just as we are protected inside a palace by the various gates in the palace wall. The back gate is always the most vulnerable to attack. It generally remains unseen because it is so small, and it is the place from which most enemies attack. If each gate is a noble quality of the heart, Lord Krishna says that this gate must always be protected by humility. If we do not have humility, all the other gates are vulnerable.

Actually, if we have the qualities of humility and simplicity, we have everything; there is nothing more we need. With humility, there is unspoken respect and nobility. We offer ourselves to the world as humble and insignificant beings with an attitude of acceptance, the hallmark of love. Our lives ooze love – we speak with love, eat with love, walk with love, sleep with love, and work with love. We are filled with so much love that there is no inclination to hurt anybody's heart. We send out waves of purity and love.

Love connects and attracts. Hard-hearted people with surly faces repel grace, whereas loving hearts naturally attract grace. Let me share with you something about my second Guide, Chariji. I observed so many outstanding qualities in him, but the one that struck me most was his poise – that space or gap we mentioned in the first chapter of this book. He was never in a rush. Even when there were many people waiting to meet him, he would attend to them lovingly, one by one. He created the space for love to enter. Whatever task was given to him, he did it with love. When he cooked, there was love oozing in his activity, and even when he scolded us, he did it with poise and a lot of love.

## Love and entropy

I would also like to expand on the idea of love as the soul's gravity by exploring love as an opposing force to entropy. Entropy is the degree of disorder or randomness in any system, whether it be the universe, a child's bedroom or our inner condition. Entropy increases over time, reflecting the instability of any system when there is no energy input to keep it stable.

Our human relationships become unstable when disorder builds up during the interactions we have day-to-day, as we store more and more emotions and reactions. This creates inner disorganisation, just as a child's bedroom becomes disorganised when more and more books and clothes pile up. We need inputs to iron out the wrinkles, so that we do not harbour and store anger and resentment in our minds.

And what is the input required? It is love. With love there is acceptance. I don't mean tolerance, because tolerating someone's mistakes is a lot lower than acceptance and love. Love irons everything out. Love comes from a pure and genuine heart. Where there is love, sacrifice is natural, and we let go of everything.

This law of entropy helps us understand the need for love in all our relationships. When we are constantly in a state of love, then zero input is needed, and that is the most stable relationship we can have. There is no need for explanations.

When two people fall in love, both their hearts expand, they lose themselves in each other, and they want to do everything to make each other happy. But often it doesn't last because the reciprocity starts varying. One person becomes aware of their own needs, whereas earlier they wanted to do anything and everything for the other person. The idea of 'What about me?' arises.

Does this mean that we should not think about ourselves when we are in love? No, that is not what I mean here. We still need to focus on our own growth, which is actually a process of rising above self-centreed responses, becoming less and less concerned with personal desires, more accepting. In fact, it helps us to be in love and resonance with others.

A good life demands acceptance. It is acceptance that makes life successful. There is no perfect human being, and our imperfections collide. Rather than pointing the finger at others, first ask yourself, 'Am I perfect?' The trick is to become neutral. It is the prerequisite for taking the next step: Neither accept nor don't accept, simply come to a neutral point. When you reach that point you will find a solution. When you are looking for guidance from Nature, from God or from your Guide, first come to that neutral point and you will be steered in the right direction.

Neutrality is like lifting a burden. It allows us to let go of prejudices and preconceptions and have a clear vision. When the direction is right, the heart feels lighter.

## Love and death

Death can happen at any moment, and what does happen in that moment? Our physical body is recycled back into the atom pool, and the other two bodies, the subtle body and the soul, go to the dimension that corresponds with the energy blueprint we have created during the life we have lived.

People ask me, 'Can I purify myself at the moment of death so that my vibratory level is the highest?' but it doesn't work that way, because we cannot achieve something at the last moment. To prepare yourself for the next dimension, try to remain in a very pure, fine vibratory level – the vibration of love. The spiritual vacuum we create in our hearts then attracts the flow of divine grace toward us. In this flow, we expand infinitely in love and contract infinitely into nothingness. This is a constant process, expanding in love and contracting in insignificance. This exercise goes on and on.

## *Suggestions*

We struggle with love because in love we lose our individuality. Love is the journey from 'I' to 'we' to 'thou.' There is no 'I' in true love. Learn to let go of the ego's hold.

Meditation is the mother of constant remembrance, and constant remembrance is the mother of love. Try meditation.

How to become more loving? Purify your field of consciousness. Then you will naturally radiate love.

Love originates at the centre of your being. It is the gravity of the soul. It therefore creates stability and centreedness, and it is the antidote to entropy and instability, both within and in all our relationships.

Acceptance is the hallmark of love.